# Virginia Climber's Guide

# VIRGINIA CLIMBER'S GUIDE

Jeff Watson

STACKPOLE
BOOKS

*To my wife, Carol*

Copyright © 1998 by Stackpole Books

Published by
STACKPOLE BOOKS
5067 Ritter Road
Mechanicsburg, PA 17055

All rights reserved, including the right to reproduce this book or portions thereof in any form or by any means, electronic or mechanical, including photocopying, recording, or by any information storage and retrieval system, without permission in writing from the publisher. All inquiries should be addressed to Stackpole Books, 5067 Ritter Road, Mechanicsburg, PA 17055.

Printed in the United States

First edition

10 9 8 7 6 5 4 3 2 1

*Cover photo of Little Stony Man Cliffs by Jeff Watson*
*Cover design by Wendy Reynolds*

**Library of Congress Cataloging-in-Publication Data**

Watson, Jeff, 1965-
    Virginia climber's guide / by Jeff Watson. — 1st ed.
       p.   cm.
    Includes bibliographical references (p. ).
    ISBN 0-8117-2981-8
    1. Rock climbing—Virginia—Guidebooks.  2. Virginia—Guidebooks.
    I. Title.
GV199.42.V8238    1998
917.5504'43—dc21                                          97-23337
                                                                                CIP

# • IMPORTANT NOTE TO READERS •

Rock climbing is an inherently dangerous sport that can result in serious injury or death. This book is intended as a guide to climbing areas in Virginia; reading it in no way guarantees your personal safety. Nor can the author or publisher be responsible for errors in directions or route descriptions.

Anyone using this book should remember the following:

1. This guidebook is not a substitute for climbing instruction. Do not attempt the climbs in this book without adequate professional instruction.

2. This guidebook is not a substitute for personal judgment. Each climber must weigh the risks of a climb against his or her own abilities.

3. The difficulty ratings in this guidebook are subjective, as are all climbing ratings. This is especially true of lesser-known climbs that have not been rated by many climbers and so lack the benefit of consensus. Ratings may be inconsistent from site to site, and a route may be more difficult than its rating. The ratings given here are intended only as a general guide.

4. Some of the directions and route information in this guidebook may contain inaccurate or misleading information. Although the author has researched the sites through multiple sources, first-hand verification of each one was impossible.

5. Although the author has made every attempt to include only those climbing areas on public land, ownership is always subject to change. Furthermore, a public area may border private property. It is therefore the responsibility of every climber to check the current status of an area and to avoid trespassing. This guide does not grant anyone the right to use private property.

The editor and publisher offer no warranty that the information in this guidebook is accurate. The use of this book as a climbing guide indicates the reader's understanding of these limitations, and further, that climbing safety is the sole responsibility of the climber.

# • CONTENTS •

Acknowledgments — ix

## Part I
## INTRODUCTION

General Information — 3
   Virginia Climbing Areas Map — 6
   Shenandoah National Park/Skyline Drive
   Climbing Areas Map — 7
Virginia Ethics — 9

## Part II
## NORTHERN VIRGINIA

1. Great Falls — 15
2. Boucher Rocks, Eagle Rock, Quaking Aspen — 37
3. Crescent Rocks — 46

## Part III
## SKYLINE DRIVE AND SHENANDOAH NATIONAL PARK

4. Fort Windham Rocks, Compton Peak — 51
5. Mount Marshall, Gravel Springs Cliff, Indian Run Rocks — 58
6. Big Devils Stairs, Little Devils Stairs, Overall Run Falls — 63
7. Marys Rock, The Pinnacles — 77
8. Little Stony Man Cliffs, Crescent Rocks — 89
9. White Oak Canyon Cliffs — 97
10. Old Rag Mountain, Rose River Falls — 140
11. Cedar Run Falls, Half-Mile Cliff — 152
12. Hawksbill Summit, Franklin Cliffs — 162
13. Blackrock, Split Rock, Lewis Falls — 172
14. Bearfence Mountain, South River Falls — 183
15. Loft Mountain, Calvary Rocks, Chimney Rocks — 190

## Part IV
## GEORGE WASHINGTON NATIONAL FOREST

| | | |
|---|---|---|
| 16 | Elizabeth Furnace Areas: Talking Headwall, Buzzard Rocks (Little El Cap) | 197 |
| 17 | Hone Quarry | 206 |
| 18 | Chimney Rock | 214 |
| 19 | Big Schloss, Little Schloss | 216 |
| 20 | Iron Gate, Clifton Forge, Low Moor | 225 |
| 21 | Crabtree Falls, Pedlar District | 230 |
| 22 | Raven's Roost, Love Gap, White Rocks, Twenty-Minute Cliff, Humpback Rock | 242 |
| 23 | McAfee's Knob, Dragon's Tooth, Eagle Rock | 254 |

## Part V
## THOMAS JEFFERSON NATIONAL FOREST

| | | |
|---|---|---|
| 24 | White Face, Fool's Face | 267 |
| 25 | Wytheville Cliff (Marion Cliff) | 268 |
| 26 | Little Stoney Creek Cliffs | 270 |

## Part VI
## STATE PARKS AND MISCELLANEOUS AREAS

| | | |
|---|---|---|
| 27 | Grayson Highlands | 275 |
| 28 | Moorman's Boulders | 280 |
| 29 | Tunstall's Tooth | 288 |
| 30 | Goshen Pass Area | 290 |

| | | |
|---|---|---|
| Appendix A | Other Possible Areas | 297 |
| Appendix B | Rules, Regulations, Addresses, YDS Rating System, and Other Useful Information | 299 |
| Bibliography | | 304 |

# · ACKNOWLEDGMENTS ·

This type of book is impossible to write without the help of a great number of people, but any mistakes and errors are strictly my fault. I would like to thank the following people:

- Everyone I climb with, but especially my regular climbing partners Chris Lundeen, Shelly Wright, and Chris "Off Belay" Sande
- Native friends Victor Todd, Pam Baumann, Hunter Allen, Steve Amuz, and Chris Taylor
- All the people at Stackpole Books, including Sally Atwater, David Uhler, Larry Johnson, Mark Allison, and Jon Rounds
- Rick Dotson and the PATC
- The guys at the Baileys Crossroads REI
- My dad, who started showing me these areas at an early age
- And my sons, Thomas and Neil, who will pass my climbing achievements any day now

# PART I

# Introduction

# General Information

## WHY VIRGINIA?

Virginia never gets the respect it deserves as an area rich in climbs. Many climbers are passing up a huge variety of climbs to crowd into the popular areas on the East Coast. Every weekend, people drive past dozens of excellent areas only to wait in line at Great Falls Park for the opportunity to climb. While climbers sign in at Seneca, dozens of routes across the state see no traffic at all. Even in-state climbers often give short shrift to these areas. Perhaps they do not know what awaits them or they have accepted the idea that nothing is there.

This project began when I was visiting some relatives in the Afton Mountain area. I had last climbed there in the late seventies and was looking for a guide to the area. A nearby bike/climbing shop offered only the Great Falls Guide and told me that there was no good climbing in the state. "What about Clifton Forge, Tunstall's Tooth, or the White Oak Canyon?" I offered. The salesperson just shrugged his shoulders. I'll let you in on a few secrets: There is good climbing in Virginia. Except for the Tidewater region, there is climbable rock everywhere. This state has a large number of national parks, national forests, and state parks. Appalachian Trail hikers spend more time passing through Virginia than any other state. Why does this matter? Because it is legal to climb in all these areas. Virginia does not have the horrific access problems that plague other areas. If you need a comparison, just talk to any climber in

Pennsylvania. Tell a Pennsylvanian climber that you are working on a guide to his area and you will receive phone threats at work. Virginia has all types of rocks from granite to sandstone. Virginia has cliffs up to 120 feet in height. Many winters are severe enough to form great ice routes in places such as White Oak Canyon and Crabtree Falls.

## PURPOSE OF THIS BOOK

Guidebooks in general have gotten a bad rap. Many fear that guidebooks are destructive forces that bring (gasp) outsiders to areas. These outsiders finish projects, chop holds, and eventually lead to the area being closed. This is nonsense. No one is going to waste time driving to an area for the purpose of ruining it. Outsiders have the same impact on an area as the locals do. A book by itself can only publicize an area; it requires abuse to ruin it.

This book's intent is to provide a listing of areas and routes for climbing. It is not within the scope of this book to give any actual advice or instruction on the techniques of climbing. Climbing is an inherently dangerous sport, and beginners should seek appropriate instruction from qualified climbers.

This is not a perfect guide. Many routes are not listed, because in researching the climbs, I found thousands of route names missing, incomplete, or wrong. I left out much first ascent information due to conflicting or missing information. Many areas have obscure guides, such as photocopied sheets handed out by store employees to whoever they think deserves them. I avoided using these single-source guides unless I could track down the original author and gain permission, because a single source of information is weak on reliability.

What are the criteria for a route name to appear in this book? The route name has to (1) have appeared in one or more publications or (2) be well known enough that its name is familiar to the majority of people climbing in the area. The correct route name depends on its being recorded. Past climbs that do not get recorded end up being mistaken for other routes, renamed, or forgotten. Their names change as others climb in the area.

Don't feel as if you should limit yourself to the routes in this book. There are many possible variations and other routes that are not mentioned. Many new climbers I meet around Great Falls treat their guidebooks as the Gospel and never consider trying anything else. A guidebook is just that—a guide. If something isn't rated or isn't in the book, give it a go anyway. You never know.

My goal was not to write a tome listing every chunk of rock in the state, but rather to show East Coast climbers that there are more challenging, less crowded, and simply better areas than the ones they wait in line to climb in.

## HOW TO USE THIS BOOK

On page 6 is a map of the state of Virginia. The map numbers refer to the individual climbing areas. Thus area #1 is Great Falls Park, and information concerning the climbs in this park can be found in Chapter 1. Following the state map is a map of the Skyline Drive section of Shenandoah National Park. Each chapter is set up the following way:

**Name.** The name or names of various cliffs or areas within the specific area.

**Description.** A brief description of the amount of climbable rock in the area. To attempt to strike a balance between the different types of climbing, this opening description gives you a good idea of the height, difficulty, and amount of rock. As someone who can spend the whole day bouldering on a 15-foot slab, I believe that any area has some worth, but I recognize that no one wants to drive to an unworthwhile area. Some climbs are fine if you live in the area, attend school in the area, or are passing through. Read the descriptions before setting out on a pilgrimage, and you won't be disappointed.

**Directions.** Specific directions to the area and, if needed, a map providing further explanation. I still recommend that you have a good map of the state or be familiar with the area. Skyline Drive and the Blue Ridge Parkway are both marked by mileposts every mile. If this guide says to park at Skyline Drive mile marker 16.3, this is an approximation. There is no mile post 16.3. Simply drive three-tenths of a mile past the mile post 16.

**Drawing of the Cliffs.** These are schematic and do not show every feature on the cliff. I used sketches instead of photos to avoid obstructions such as trees and to avoid the worm's-eye/bird's-eye view issue. Sketches can show multiplanar surfaces better than

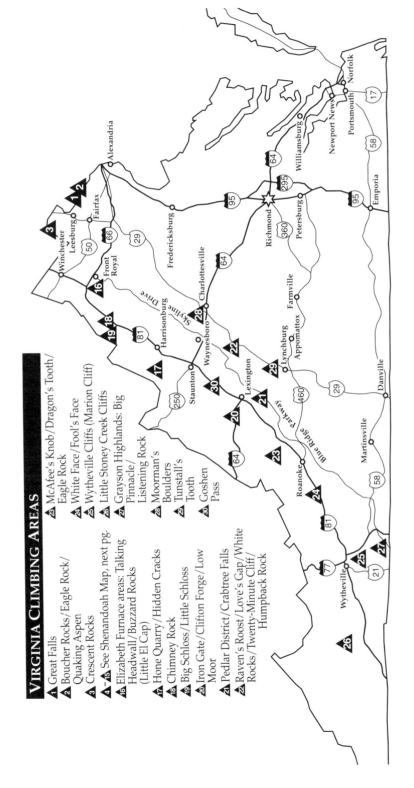

## CLIMBING AREAS
### Shenandoah National Park/Skyline Drive

- **4** Fort Windham Rocks/Compton Peak/Gooney Creek Cliffs
- **5** Mount Marshall/Gravel Springs Cliff/Indian Run
- **6** Big Devils Stairs/Little Devils Stairs/Overall Run Falls
- **7** Marys Rock/The Pinnacles
- **8** Little Stony Man Cliffs
- **9** White Oak Canyon
- **10** Old Rag Mountain/Rose River Falls
- **11** Cedar Run Falls/Half-mile Cliff
- **12** Hawksbill Summit/Franklin Cliffs
- **13** Blackrock/Split Rock/Lewis Falls
- **14** Bearfence Mountain/South River Cliffs
- **15** Loft Mountain/Calvary Rocks/Chimney Rocks

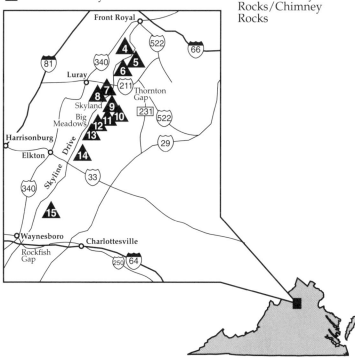

photographs. The bottom line is that sketches can depict the cliff more accurately. Known routes and possible routes are marked by dotted lines and are numbered. Areas with multiple cliffs or with cliffs spread out over a general area are in the order that you will come to them unless otherwise noted.

**Route Descriptions.** The route descriptions include the following:
- The name or names of the route. Please remember that names change over the years as climbers discover and rediscover the climbs. Every effort has been made to discover the "correct" name.
- The rating. Ratings are given in the Yosemite Decimal Scale (see Appendix B, p. 303). Please remember that these ratings are subjective.
- The maximum height of the route. The cliff might be taller.
- A brief description of the route. This description is to ensure that the climber can follow the route correctly.
- Variations.

**Nearby Areas.** I've included other nearby areas not large enough or usable enough to warrant their own chapters and/or nearby bouldering areas. Why include areas that do not warrant a visit? I tend to spend a lot of time scouring over maps, often at my boss's expense, making plans to visit areas. A listing on a map, such as Bettys Rock, would become an undiscovered Trango Tower in my mind. Outside my imagination, Bettys Rock is a low-angle 8-foot boulder, unsuitable for any type of climbing. A listing for Bettys Rock at the end of a chapter allows you to steer clear of this area.

**Other Information.** This includes where to park, nearby camping options, park regulations, any applicable fees, first ascents, and anything else of special interest. General information on parks is in Appendix B.

# Virginia Ethics

Every guidebook has one of these sections, and it generally either preaches a sermon or issues a few clichés: "The earth is like your mother's house, and you wouldn't throw Power Bar wrappers on your mother's floor, would you?" This might be a fitting analogy, but it doesn't do anything about the problems caused by climbing.

Climbers always claim that the trash around sites comes from locals, fishermen, and campers. Landowners always blame the group that they are least familiar with. Climbers probably are not throwing condoms, Stroh's cans, and Skoal tins on the ground, but I do suspect that climbers are responsible for the Power Bar wrappers, finger tape, and carpet squares. At any rate, climbers are going to get blamed for everything. Landowners will never admit that it's the local high schoolers (their kids) or local hunters (their buddies) who are causing the problems.

What to do? This problem requires a new way of viewing the situation. Look at it this way: Every climbing area in Virginia is on the verge of being closed. Any combination of littering, accidents, and trespassing brings us closer to the day when outdoor climbing is banned. If you doubt this, just talk to someone associated with the Access Fund. Even the national parks, which on the East Coast have not had to develop serious climbing policies, can close off areas. This is preventable, and here are my suggestions to help keep areas open:

**Don't Trespass.** This is the biggest problem that landowners have with climbers. I have made every attempt to include only areas on public lands, but that status can change at any time. Check with a group such as the Access Fund to keep up with access issues. In Virginia, you can contact the Access Fund's local representatives. If every indication is that the area is open but you run into a "No Trespassing" sign, go somewhere else. Often, you can find the landowner and ask permission. I've never had a landowner turn me down when asked directly. Here are some sure signs that you are trespassing: (1) You are by a railroad or a quarry, (2) you are by a "No Trespassing" sign, or (3) you have to climb a fence to get to the area. In short, avoid climbing next to highways, and remember that it's almost always trespassing to walk along railroad tracks. Parking your car by a driveway or a "No Parking" sign is a form of trespass and makes landowners mad.

**Don't Litter.** Put your Power Bar wrappers in your pack and throw them away at home. Put your muddy carpet square in your trunk. Leaving it at the crag not only looks bad, but it's worthless when it gets wet. Fingertape balls do not biodegrade; take them home. Cigarette butts are also litter. Don't throw them on the ground; pack them out. Carry a trash bag in your pack and take away a couple of pieces of other people's trash. Clean areas tend to stay clean, and trashy areas just keep getting dirtier. Besides, picking up other's trash will give you that superior feeling that so many climbers have anyway.

**Respect the Traditions of the Area.** I've climbed almost everywhere in the state, and I've seen only a few bolts. Let's leave it that way. I'll also go out on a limb and say that chipping holds is wrong. Maybe unclimbable faces should exist. These could be the 5.16s of the future, but if they are all chipped into 5.13s, we'll never know.

**Be Safe.** This is most important. Be extra careful around waterfall areas, as many people die every year tumbling over falls. Remember that ice climbing this far south is chancy and depends on the correct weather conditions. When in doubt, phone ahead to the rangers. Great Falls Park, the crag closest to my house and 15 million others, is severely overcrowded. Two or three times a year, a death is attributed to climbing. Usually it is teenagers scrambling on the cliff faces or a beginner free-soloing. This park scares me. For example: Here you can see 14-year-olds with $2,000 racks and no experience struggling to top-rope 5.3 cracks with suspect belaying at best. A climber from an out-of-state college asked me if the overhand knot was a water knot. I showed her the proper knot, and she proceeded to turn around and begin teaching a climbing class. A 200-pound military guy jumped from the top of a cliff to see if his 125-pound girlfriend could belay him. "I have to know if I can trust you," he yelled. "I don't think this is a good idea," she screamed back. A group of rappelers saw the care we took with our rope and asked if it was okay to keep their rope in the garage with gas and paint cans. It has become easy to walk into a store and buy equipment and instructional books and head to the rocks. Please do yourself and everyone else a favor by learning to climb responsibly. This involves instruction from a qualified instructor, not a book or a video.

# PART II

# Northern Virginia

# • CHAPTER 1 •

# Great Falls

Great Falls, a deep canyon along the Potomac River, has more routes than any other climbing area in the state. However, on any nice weekend, you will have a hard time finding a place to climb. The combination of its proximity to the Washington, D.C., area and its dearth of routes is its downfall. Great Falls is an area where the Potomac Appalachian Trail Club has diligently recorded every first ascent and route name over the years. Routes can reach 60 feet in height. Remember that some of these routes vanish in times of high water.

Follow the rules while climbing at Great Falls. Do not climb in the canal cut. It is a protected historical site. Remember to sign in at the board. Signing in is not Big Brother watching you, but rather a way to show that climbing is one of the major activities at the park.

I suspect that the government is considering banning or seriously reducing climbing in this park. In the past five years, the number of inexperienced climbers fooling around on difficult routes without proper anchors and belays has increased. Accidents and deaths have increased. True, any tourist falling off a cliff is called a climber in the statistics, but the impact is the same. Climb safely wherever you choose to climb, but pay special attention to your activities while at Great Falls Park.

## DIRECTIONS

Reach Great Falls Park by going north on congested I-495 and then going west on 193 (Georgetown Pike). Follow Georgetown Pike and turn onto road 738, Old Dominion Drive. After 1 mile, you'll be at the front gate. Take the immediate right after the gate and drive to the end. This is the climbers' and kayakers' parking lot (not really, so don't yell at the picnickers who park here). Once again, remember to sign in at the climber's board, located at the end of the parking area. There are also some other parking areas at trailheads along route 193 that lead into the park.

## ROUTE DESCRIPTIONS

Arriving at these various areas takes some searching and backtracking. The trails along the cliff tops are a series of mazes. When this guide states that you should go upstream or downstream from one area to another, this is not a literal directive. Sometimes (often depending on the current river height), it is possible to travel from area to area along the river's edge. More often than not, you have to ascend and descend the cliffs by a walkdown to reach other areas. Be particularly careful when traveling up or down the walkdown areas. If you are in a hurry to reach an area or burned out, your concentration is probably at its lowest, and it is very easy to get injured falling off a 70-foot 5.0. Additionally, as climbing injuries go, it is always embarrassing to admit that you fell off a snack bar deck, ladder, or walkdown. Not all the recorded or possible routes are listed. Consider this a mere sampling of the possibilities.

By following the path from the parking area, you will come to Mather's Gorge and Area A.

## AREA A: THE DIHEDRALS

Located directly under the plaque dedicated to Stephen Mather. The climbs are listed upstream to downstream.

1. **Skink 5.8, 50 ft.**
   Climb the overhang, staying to the right.

2. **Take Five 5.5, 50 ft.**
   Starting below the overhang, climb the center of the wall.

3   **Smash 5.9, 50 ft.**
    Climb the overhang, staying to the left.

4   **The Crypt 5.3, 22 ft.**
    Climb the corner.

5   **Stop the Presses 5.11, 60 ft.**
    Climb the left crack, the overhang, and the upper wall.

6   **Die-hedral 5.10, 60 ft.**
    Climb the ramp and dihedral, avoiding the edge.

7   **Executioner's Song 5.8, 60 ft.**
    Climb the dihedral.

8   **Rest in Piece 5.6, 60 ft.**
    Climb the ledges to the dihedral.

9   **Chimney 45 ft.**
    Climb the easy chimney.

10  **Lichen Wall 5.3–5.7, 60 ft.**
    Climb anywhere on this wall.

11  **Prejudice 5.5, 60 ft.**
    Climb the dihedral.

12  **Pride** (Do I sense a Jane Austen motif?) **5.4, 60 ft.**
    Climb the hand crack.

13  **Ender 5.11, 55 ft.**
    Climb the crack.

14  **Layback 5.4, 50 ft.**
    Layback the dihedral directly under Mather's plaque.

15  **The Roll 5.11, 50 ft.**
    Climb the corner and the overhang.

16  **Jay's Discover 5.1, 45 ft.**
    Climb the easy dihedral.

By heading upstream from Mather's Gorge, you will find Area B.

## DIHEDRALS

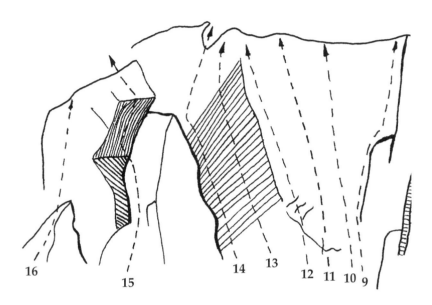

### AREA B: SAND BOX AND FLAT IRON

The climbs are listed as you head downstream to upstream.

17  Sand Box Corner 5.4, 45 ft.
    Climb the easy corner.

18  The Pox 5.7, 45 ft.
    Climb the face.

19  Sand Castles 5.6, 45 ft.
    Climb the corner.

20  Flat Iron Corner 5.5, 25 ft.
    Climb the cracks on the corner.

21  Bikini Corner 5.7, 40 ft.
    Climb the corner.

## DIHEDRALS

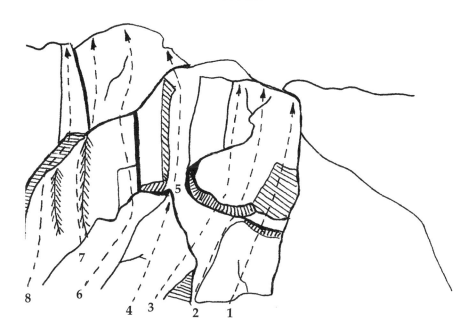

## SANDBOX

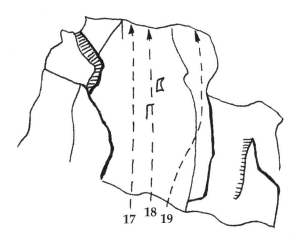

## FLAT IRON

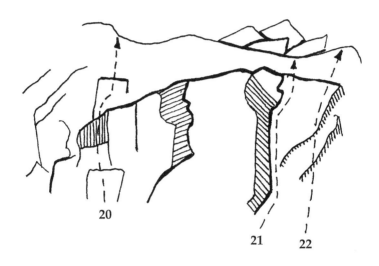

22  **Bikini 5.5, 40 ft.**
    Climb the leaning face.

Upstream from Flat Iron is Area C.

### AREA C: MICRODOME

The climbs are still listed going downstream to upstream.

23  **B-29 5.6, 40 ft.**
    Climb the deep crack.

24  **B-52 5.9, 40 ft.**
    Climb the leaning corner.

25  **M-1 5.10, 40 ft.**
    Do the overhang and climb the upper cracks. Variation: Same rating, but stay to the right after finishing the overhang. It is also possible to traverse right under the overhang.

Starting over again from Mather's Gorge, but heading downstream, you will find Area D.

## MICRODOME

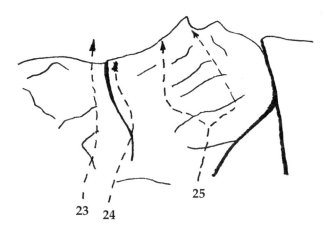

## AREA D: DIKE CREEK

26  **Chockstone Chimney 5.6, 25 ft.**
    Climb the chimney.

27  **Wet Bottom 5.3, 25 ft.**
    Climb the crack.

28  **Glass Corner 5.5, 30 ft.**
    Climb the corner separating the dike inlet from the Potomac.

29  **Broken Glass 5.2, 25 ft.**
    Climb any of the cracks.

30  **Epigone 5.6, 25 ft.**
    On the upper ledge, climb the jam crack.

31  **Sciolist 5.10, 25 ft.**
    Climb the crack to the left of Epigone. (A sciolist is someone who displays superficial knowledge, oops.)

## DIKE CREEK

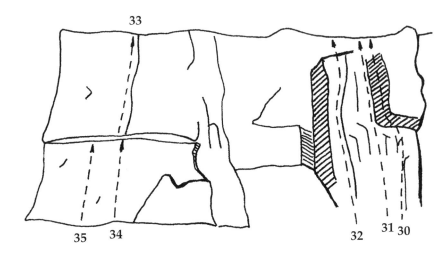

32  **Mantelpiece 5.10, 50 ft.**
    A Great Falls classic. Climb the thin face, avoiding the corner and the edge.

The next three climbs are on a 15-foot-wide ledge that is mistakenly called Juliet's Balcony.

33  **Right Stuff 5.7, 35 ft.**
    On the upper ledge, climb the hand crack. Variation: Left Stuff—climb the face, staying out of the crack.

34  **Backslider 5.7, 30 ft.**
    On the lower face, climb the crack.

35  **Possibilities 5.9, 30 ft.**
    Climb the thin crack on the downstream side of the lower face.

Past Dike Creek, still going downstream, is Area E.

## DIKE CREEK

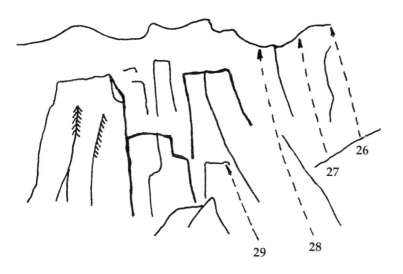

### AREA E: JULIET'S BALCONY CLIFFS

36  Seclusion 5.7, 50 ft.
    Climb the crack.

37  Zig-zag Edge 5.5, 50 ft.
    Climb the crack, remembering to zigzag onto the two faces.

38  Stan's Lead 5.5, 50 ft.
    Climb the corner and overhang.

39  Sickle Face 5.10, 50 ft.
    Climb the face.

40  Snowflake 5.6, 50 ft.
    Climb the crack in the inside corner.

41  Flaky 5.8, 52 ft.
    Climb the overhang over the flaky face.

42  Great Beginnings 5.7, 55 ft.
    Follow the cracks up and climb the corner.

## JULIET'S BALCONY

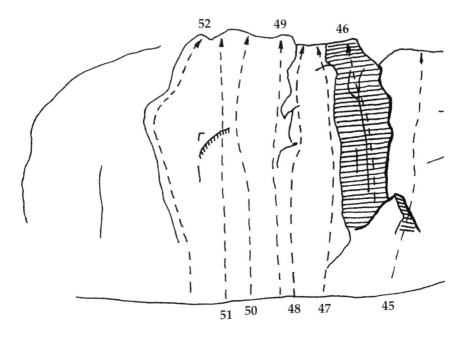

43 **Nylon's 5.9, 45 ft.**
Climb the outcropping face.

44 **Juliet's Balcony 5.1, 50 ft.**
Believe it or not, this is the real Juliet's Balcony. Follow the gently sloping face.

45 **Romeo's Retreat**
Beginner's wall. Used for teaching classes, this is one of the scariest areas in the park. It is amazing what passes for instruction.

46 **Romeo's Ladder 5.6, 35 ft.**
A Great Falls classic. Climb the cracks; the left crack is the hardest route. There are several variations.

47 **Ergometer 5.11, 35 ft.**
Climb the microholds around the corner from Romeo's Ladder.

## JULIET'S BALCONY

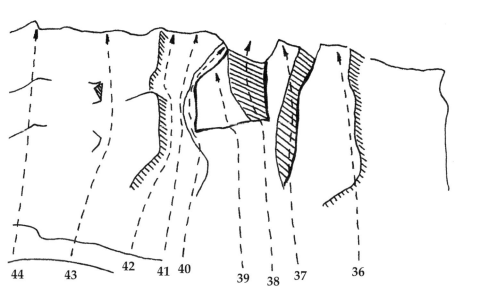

48 **Lunging Ledges 5.9, 40 ft.**
   Climb the face.

49 **Entropy 5.10+, 45 ft.**
   Climb the face to the overhang and head left.

50 **Demon 5.12, 45 ft.**
   Climb the face to the crack.

51 **Oyster 5.11+, 45 ft.**
   Follow the thin flake.

52 **Delivery Room 5.5, 45 ft.**
   Climb the jam crack.

Even farther downstream is Area F.

## AID BOX

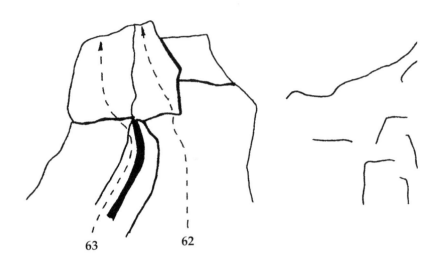

63   62

## AREA F: AID BOX

*Note:* The canal cut is in this area. It is a protected historical site, and climbing here is a sure way to be thrown out of the park.

53   **Potomac Valley Wall 5.11, 25 ft.**
     Climb the leaning face and avoid the crack.

54   **Potomac Valley Overhang 5.12, 30 ft.**
     Good roof problem.

55   **The Strain 5.12, 35 ft.**
     Traverse the wall and ascend by way of the thin crack.

56   **Lost Arrow or Terrapin Station 5.10, 35 ft.**
     Climb the crack.

57   **Splinters 5.7, 35 ft.**
     Climb the corner.

58   **The Box 5.5, 40 ft.**
     Climb the corner.

## AID BOX

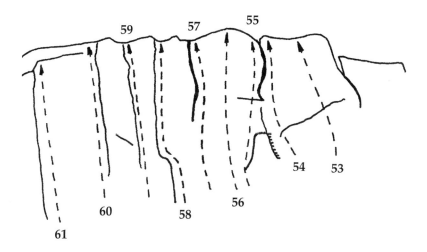

59  **Diagonal 5.8, 40 ft.**
    Climb the crack.

60  **Monkey Fingers 5.12, 40 ft.**
    Climb the finger crack.

61  **Dark Corner 5.6, 40 ft.**
    Climb the corner.

The next two routes are usually vacant on weekends. They are just up from the canal cut.

62  **Foops Junior 5.10-, 30 ft.**
    Climb the chimney and overhang.

63  **Grimsome Wall 5.7, 40 ft.**
    Climb the wide crack.

At the canal cut it is okay to climb the following walls since they face the river. The inner walls are a historical site.

## AID BOX

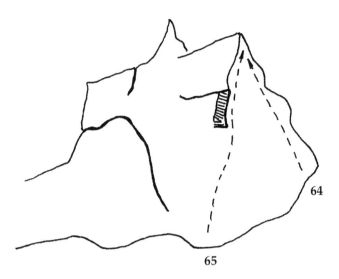

64 **Monster Manly 5.9, 55 ft.**
Climb the leaning face and quartz overhang.

65 **Hercules 5.9, 55 ft.**
Follow the crack around the overhang.

Head downstream to Area G.

## AREA G: BIRD'S NEST

After all the Byrd's Nests in Shenandoah Park, it's nice to see a Bird's Nest.

66 **Eagle's Nest 5.9, 50 ft.**
Climb the corner and the mild overhang.

67 **Fair Square 5.11, 50 ft.**
Climb the bulging edge.

68 **Bird's Nest 5.7, 60 ft.**
Climb the corner and avoid the large overhang to the right. Variation: 5.12; climb the center of the roof.

69  **Two Lane Highway 5.10, 40 ft.**
    Climb the face and avoid the roof by heading left.

70  **One Lane Highway 5.10, 40 ft.**
    Climb the face and follow the crack.

71  **Shoulder of the Road** (I'll say one thing for these 1940–50 climbers: when they pick a motif, they stay with it) **5.9, 60 ft.**
    Climb the bumpy edge.

72  **The Man's Route 5.8, 60 ft.**
    Starting downstream of the Shoulder, climb the jam crack.

73  **Lightning Bolt 5.11, 50 ft.**
    Climb the Z-shaped crack.

74  **Armbuster 5.9, 45 ft.**
    Climb the classic overhang.

75  **The Nose 5.6, 50 ft.**
    Climb the overhang and follow the crack.

76  **Cranko 5.10, 60 ft.**
    Climb either the right or the left crack.

77  **Tiparillo 5.11+, 60 ft.**
    A traverse problem leading to a small overhang.

78  **Cornice 5.7, 55 ft.**
    Climb the overhangs. Variation: 5.9; follow the finger crack.

79  **Lawrence's Last 5.1, 50 ft.**
    Climb the easy crack.

80  **Darius Green's Flying Machine 5.10, 50 ft.**
    Climb the edge.

81  **Conroy Wasn't Here 5.7, 45 ft.**
    Climb the corner.

82  **Inclined Plane 5.7, 60 ft.**
    Climb the inclined plane and follow the crack.

## BIRD'S NEST

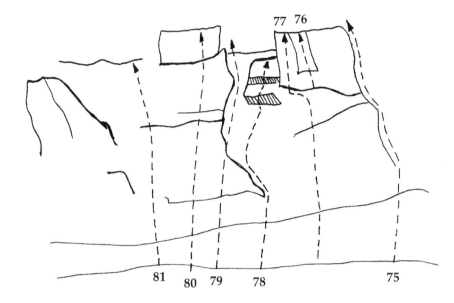

83  **A Bridge Too Far 5.10, 55 ft.**
    Climb the corner and the overhang.

84  **Conroy 5.7, 60 ft.**
    Climb the cracks and overhang.

85  **Balder 5.4, 45 ft.**
    Climb the easy corner.

86  **Wall of Da Feet 5.6–5.8, 35 ft.**
    Climb anywhere on this wall.

87  **Needlepoint Corner 5.3, 40 ft.**
    Climb the inner corner.

88  **Dr. Needlepoint 5.9, 40 ft.**
    Climb the cracks.

89  **Blitzkrieg 5.11, 40 ft.**
    Climb the edge to the left of Dr. Needlepoint.

## BIRD'S NEST

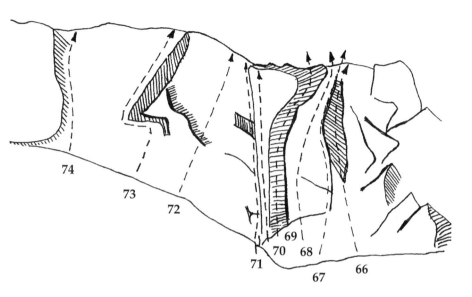

90  **Poison Ivy Face 5.5–5.7, 50 ft.**
    Climb anywhere on the face.

91  **Last Exit 5.6, 50 ft.**
    Climb the crack.

92  **Backstretch 5.10, 50 ft.**
    Climb the face to the right of the overhang.

93  **Degree 101 5.11, 50 ft.**
    Climb the overhang.

94  **Corkscrew 5.4, 50 ft.**
    Climb the corner.

95  **Con-cave 5.10, 35 ft.**
    Climb the leaning face.

96  **Dingo 5.2, 35 ft.**
    Follow the large crack.

## BIRD'S NEST

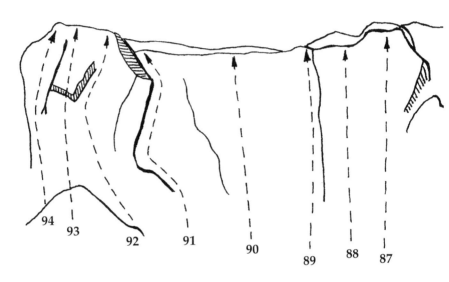

## BIRD'S NEST

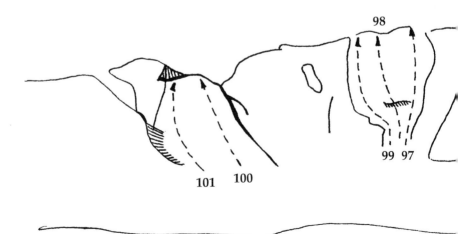

Great Falls • 33

## BIRD'S NEST

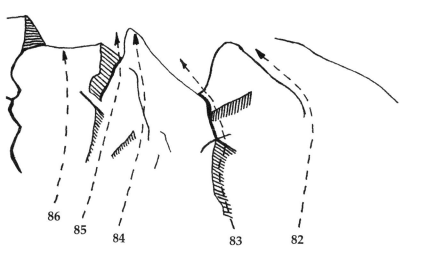

## BIRD'S NEST

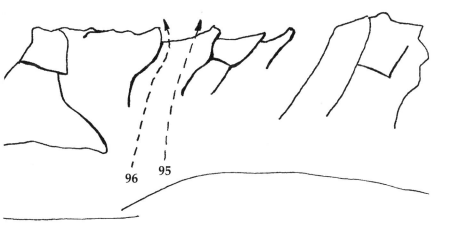

97   **Waldorf Astoria 5.11, 50 ft.**
     Climb the face to the left of Dingo.

98   **The Jug 5.9, 50 ft.**
     Climb the overhang and head right.

99   **Nelson's Nemesis 5.7, 50 ft.**
     Follow the cracks.

100  **The Silver Scream 5.10, 50 ft.**
     Climb the face.

101  **The Insignificant One 5.9, 50 ft.**
     Climb the corner just downstream from The Silver Scream.

From this point on, the cliff begins to peter out, but there are still some good beginner routes.

## AREA H: COW'S HOOF AND ECHO ROCK

These climbs are so far downstream that it's easier to reach the area by parking at the Difficult Run Parking Area along Route 193. Follow the same directions to the park, but before reaching Old Dominion Drive, you'll see the Difficult Run Parking Area. The climbs are listed from upstream to downstream.

102  **Caliban 5.8, 35 ft.**
     Climb the corner. Variation: Climb the face on the left.

103  **Claws 5.12, 40 ft.**
     Climb the leaning face.

104  **Socrates' Downfall 5.8, 40 ft.**
     Layback the crack under the Hemlock (do you get it?).

105  **Hard Nut 5.12+, 40 ft.**
     Climb the very thin crack.

106  **Hemlock 5.10, 35 ft.**
     Climb the corner downstream from Socrates' Downfall.

107  **F.I.S.T. 5.9, 50 ft.**
     Climb the crack.

## COW'S HOOF

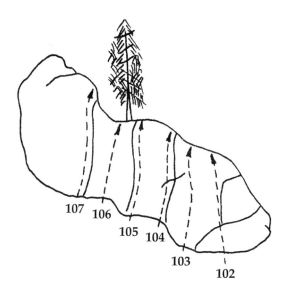

Echo Rock is a dirty cliff located downstream from the cliffs at Cow's Hoof. Several traverses can be done, and it's a good cliff for practicing some leads. Echo Rock is not pictured.

### NEARBY AREAS

Carderock is located nearby. It is a classic area for local climbers with routes of all grades up to 50 feet in height. Reach it on I-495 North by crossing the Chain Bridge into Maryland and taking the first exit. Stay to your left and take Canal Road northwest. Follow the signs to the Carderock Recreation Area. Park in the farthest parking area and follow the path. Carderock is famous for the dozens of people who walk around critiquing your climbing and yelling out route information. Avoid the area on weekends, if possible.

You can reach the Maryland side of Great Falls by heading toward Carderock, but passing by the recreation area. When Canal Road intersects MacArthur Boulevard, follow the sign to Great Falls Park. The cliffs are down the C&O Canal Towpath across from the cliffs on the Virginia side.

Also, check out everything in Chapter 2.

## OTHER INFORMATION

No swimming in the Potomac, no alcoholic beverages, no camping, and no glass allowed. As mentioned earlier, do not climb in the canal cut or any other historical site. Climbing directly under the overlooks is illegal, plus startled tourists might drop Yoohoo bottles on you. You cannot climb between the tourist overlooks and the falls. Don't despair—even with all these restricted areas, there is still much rock to climb. Good luck.

• CHAPTER 2 •

# Boucher Rocks, Eagle Rock, Quaking Aspen

These are some good bouldering and top-rope areas close by Great Falls Park. Although these areas have less rock than Great Falls, there are also smaller crowds. These areas have challenging climbs without the wait or the close vigilance of the U.S. Park Service.

Boucher Rocks is the most established and has climbs up to 50 feet in height. Eagle Rock has cliffs up to 40 feet in height, but most of it appears to be on private property, so no routes are given. Quaking Aspen and the bouldering areas around it reach heights of 45 feet.

## DIRECTIONS

From Virginia, reach these areas by taking I-495 North to the border of Virginia and Maryland. Chain Bridge separates the states. Before you reach the bridge, take the exit for 193 and head east toward Langley. Immediately after pulling onto 193, get into the left lane and turn left onto Balls Hill Road. Head down Balls Hill and turn left at the bridge onto the seldom marked Live Oak Road. Live Oak Road ends in a cul-de-sac, and you will see a trailhead sign for the Potomac Appalachian Trail Club. Park here. Do not block the entrance to anyone's home (most of these houses are owned by Washington lawyers). Head down the trail to the river. Turning left takes you upriver through the woods to Boucher Rocks. Continuing upriver past Boucher Rocks brings you to Eagle Rock. Turning right and following the blue-blazed trail downriver brings you to a cliff called Quaking Aspen and to several good bouldering areas.

## ROUTE DESCRIPTIONS

### BOUCHER ROCKS

The climbs are listed as you come to them (from downriver to upriver).

1. **The Cracks 5.8, 45 ft.**
   This route is around the downstream side and uphill from the main cliffs at Boucher Rocks. Climb the smooth face between the two cracks.

The following are on the main face at Boucher Rocks:

2. **Seeds and Stems 5.10, 40 ft.**
   Climb the right-facing corner.

3. **Dancing Climb 5.8, 40 ft.**
   Climb the low-angle ramp. First ascent: Paul Bradt, 1946.

**BOUCHER ROCKS**

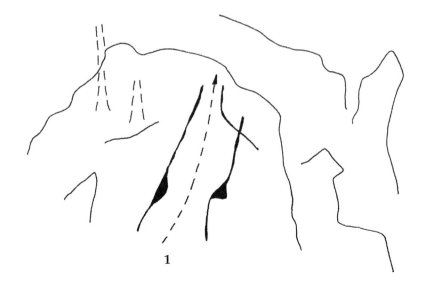

## BOUCHER ROCKS

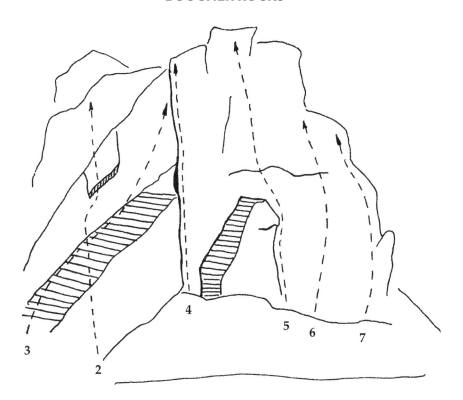

4  **Long Corner 5.8, 50 ft.**
   Climb the crack in the corner. Variations: 5.5; layback the crack; or, 5.8, climb the face to the left of the corner.

5  **Dirty Dancing 5.10, 50 ft.**
   Starting at the flake, climb the face.

6  **Dirt Wall 5.9, 50 ft.**
   Two separate routes: Climb either the crack and the face or just the face.

7  **Arch-sill 5.11, 50 ft.**
   At the most upriver edge of Boucher Rocks, climb the face.

## QUAKING ASPEN

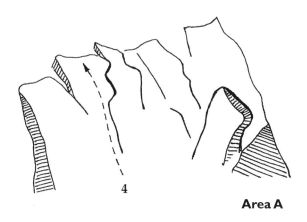

**Area A**

---

**QUAKING ASPEN**

**Area A**

On the bridge-facing side:

1  **Bolt Wall 5.8–5.10, 45 ft.**
   Hard face climbs on this wall with microholds. Several bolts have been placed on this wall over the last two summers. Are they practice bolts? This wall was once considered the place for piton practice. At any rate, bolts are not needed on this face, as it can be easily top-roped.

   On the river-facing side:

2  **5.9, 40 ft.**
   Climb the crack on the leaning face.

3  **5.4, 20 ft.**
   On the lower block, climb the face.

4  **5.6, 20 ft.**
   On the underside of climb 3, climb the crack on the leaning face.

## QUAKING ASPEN

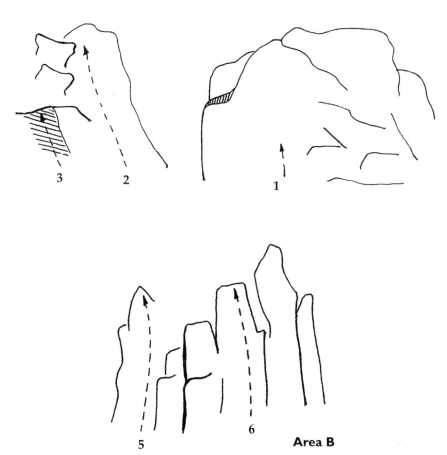

### Area B
There is good bouldering on the bridge-facing side of this 30-foot cliff.

5   **5.8, 30 ft.**
    On the farthest downriver side, climb the face.

6   **5.9, 30 ft.**
    On the river-facing side, climb the long edge of the cliff.

## Area C
On the 30-foot cliff facing the bridge:

7   5.5, 30 ft.
    Climb the crack face. Beware of loose rocks.

8   5.7, 20 ft.
    Climb the off-width crack or the leaning face.

## Area D
On the 40-foot cliff, facing the river:

9   5.4, 40 ft.
    To the right of the blocks, climb the easy ledges.

10  5.5, 40 ft.
    Climb the face by the overhanging edge.

11  5.6, 40 ft.
    Climb the long crack separating the faces.

## Area E
On the 45-foot cliff, facing the river:

12  **Truth Decay 5.7, 35 ft.**
    Starting under the jagged overhang, climb the face.

13  5.5, 30 ft.
    Avoid the overhang by heading to the left.

### NEARBY AREAS

Great Falls Park and Carderock are nearby (see Chapter 1). Prospect and Maddox Rocks are located about 3 miles upriver from Boucher Rocks. Maddox Rock has a shallow cave.

Camp Lewis is located directly across the Potomac River from Boucher Rocks. Reach it by canoeing across the river (no one recommends swimming in the Potomac). It can also be reached from the Carderock Parking Area by following the C&O Canal downriver to the second spillway. Head down the spillway toward the Potomac River. Camp Lewis is on the left. I remember this as an average area with a few nice intermediate routes. My journal has an entry that

## QUAKING ASPEN

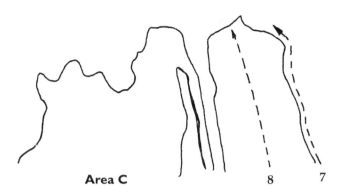

Area C

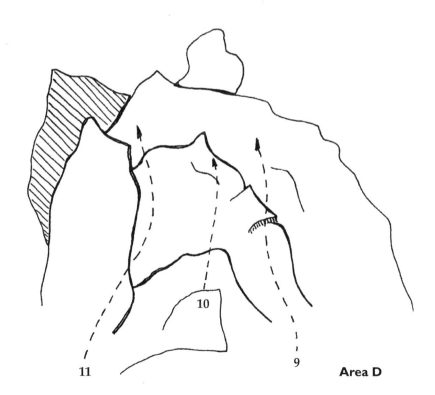

Area D

## QUAKING ASPEN

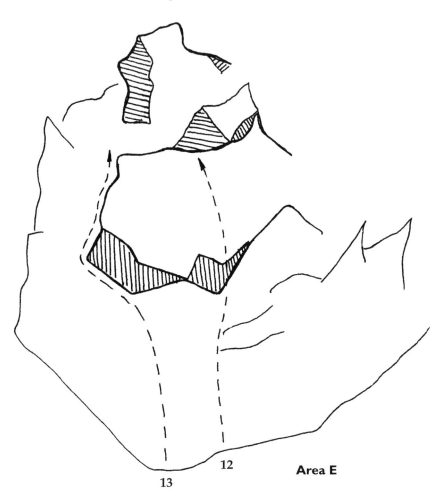

reads: "Camp Lewis; completely wet and covered with moss, yellow jackets, and sticky bushes. Nice climbs, but have head examined before climbing here again."

The islands in the middle of the Potomac River have cliffs on them. The easiest way to get to them is to launch your canoe at the Carderock Recreation Area. They are called Turkey, Herzog, and Vaso Islands.

Ripe Mango is a 70-foot cliff along the George Washington Parkway between Chain Bridge and Key Bridge. From I-395, go west on the George Washington Parkway. Park at the first overlook and walk east for about 350 yards. The cliff is below, but it will be hard to find a walkdown. The rock is very loose.

**OTHER INFORMATION**

Not much camping is available in northern Virginia. Most campgrounds, such as Burke Lake, have been closed due to the large numbers of migrant construction workers who live in the park. If you have to camp, try Bull Run Park in Manassas.

· CHAPTER 3 ·

# Crescent Rocks

Crescent Rocks is a sad case of an area being closed by disgruntled locals. I do not know who is to blame, but parking along a narrow road, trespassing, and a fire that destroyed acres of a nice valley are part of the problem. Local pressure caused a telephone company to close a popular parking lot, and Crescent Rocks is left with no good access. Until the parking area is reopened (check with the Access Fund), I don't recommend climbing here. The only other solution is hiking up the Appalachian Trail to reach the area. This adds about 6 miles (round-trip) to your hike.

## DIRECTIONS

From Leesburg, take Route 7 north past Purcellville to Snickers Gap. This is the point where the Appalachian Trail crosses Route 7. Due to the closed parking lot on Route 601, you will have to park in a park-and-ride spot on the southern end of Route 7. From this parking lot, you can head south on the Appalachian Trail, but to go to Crescent Rocks, you must head north. Cross Route 7 and walk west. The Appalachian Trail heads north behind the next green sign reading "Pine Groves". Walk up the trail 2.2 miles. On your left is the blue-blazed trail leading to Crescent Rocks. No climbs are pictured here.

## NEARBY AREAS

There are nearby climbs in West Virginia and in Maryland at Harpers Ferry. You are also 50 miles from Great Falls and other good climbing areas (see Chapters 1 and 2 for more information).

By traveling south from the commuter parking lot at Snickers Gap, you will come to the Appalachian Trail in 0.3 mile. Head south 0.3 mile to Bear Rocks, which has some good bouldering on 25-foot cliffs.

## OTHER INFORMATION

Camp along the Appalachian Trail. The top of Crescent Rocks is a good but waterless campsite. There are nearby streams, but bring your filter.

# PART III

# Skyline Drive and Shenandoah National Park

• CHAPTER 4 •

# Fort Windham Rocks, Compton Peak

Fort Windham Rocks offers good routes at all levels. Its location at the northernmost end of Skyline Drive and its short approach make it a good area for avoiding the crowds at the northern Virginia crags. Expect routes up to 35 feet in height, but beware of loose rocks on the faces.

Compton Peak cliffs are rare formations of columnar basalt. They offer two 45-foot cliffs with several good routes.

### DIRECTIONS

Reach Fort Windham Rocks by entering Skyline Drive at the Front Royal entrance and parking at Skyline Drive mile marker 10.4, the Compton Gap parking lot. Follow the marked trail 0.6 mile to a concrete post. Turn left for 0.2 mile. The rocks should be on your left.

Reach Compton Peak by crossing the drive for the Compton Gap parking lot and heading up the blue-blazed trail. After 0.8 mile, turn left at the concrete post and go down the viewpoint trail 0.2 mile.

52 • VIRGINIA CLIMBERS GUIDE

## FORT WINDHAM ROCKS AREA

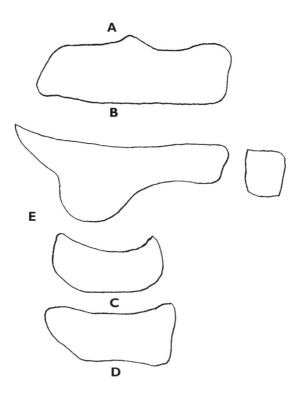

## ROUTE DESCRIPTIONS

### FORT WINDHAM ROCKS

#### Area A
On the 30-foot east-facing wall:

1  5.4–5.7, 30 ft.
   Climb anywhere on the wall. The most popular route goes up to the left of the thin crack in the center.

#### Area B
Climb the 4-foot-wide chimney (not pictured).

#### Area C
There are two cliff faces separated by 8 feet and a variety of routes ranging from 5.5–5.7 (not pictured).

#### Area D
On the east-facing cliff in the rear of the Fort Windham Rocks area:

2  5.4, 12–20 feet.
   Climb the easy face.

3  5.9, 35 ft.
   Climb the overhanging corner.

#### Area E
Around the corner from climb 4, facing south:

4  5.11, 35 ft.
   Climb the leaning slab.

5  5.12, 30 ft.
   Climb the leaning block.

#### Area F
South faces of Areas A and B:

6  5.7, 35 ft.
   Climb the right side of the face.

7  5.4, 35 ft.
   Climb the face to the right of the chimney.

## FORT WINDHAM ROCKS

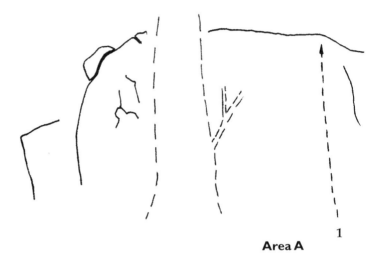

Area A

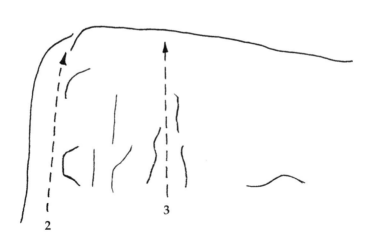

Area D

# FORT WINDHAM ROCKS

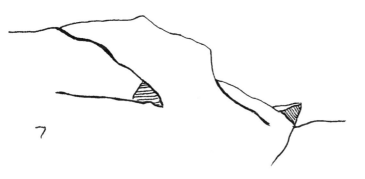

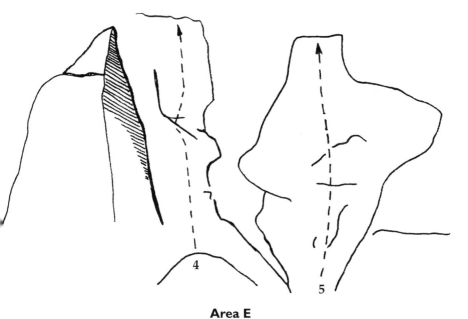

**Area E**

## FORT WINDHAM ROCKS

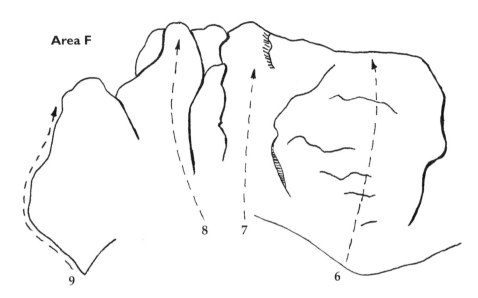

## COMPTON PEAK

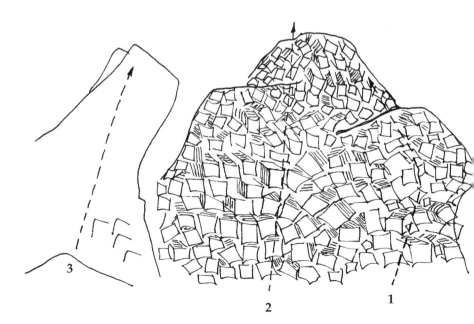

8   **5.6, 20 ft.**
    Climb the face to the left of the chimney.

9   **5.4, 15 ft.**
    Climb the far left corner.

## COMPTON PEAK

1   **5.11, 45 ft.**
    On the right corner, climb the leaning slab.

2   **5.10, 45 ft.**
    Climb the leaning face.

3   **5.7, 35 ft.**
    On the west cliff, climb the face.

### NEARBY AREAS

The Gooney Creek Cliffs are a tiny crag 200 feet below the overlook with the same name. They have little value to climbers. See other chapters for nearby areas in Shenandoah National Park. Possum's Rest is a small crag up the Appalachian Trail from Fort Windham Rocks.

### OTHER INFORMATION

Typical Shenandoah National Park regulations apply. There is good camping anywhere, but remember to get a backcountry permit and camp away from the trail.

• CHAPTER 5 •

# Mount Marshall, Gravel Springs Cliff, Indian Run Rocks

Mount Marshall (once owned by Chief Justice John Marshall) offers some good routes with a short approach from Skyline Drive. Expect cliffs from 25 to 70 feet in height.

Gravel Springs Cliff is a tiny 15-foot crag that is included only because of its proximity to the Gravel Springs camping area. The crag at Gravel Springs is not pictured.

Indian Run Rocks is a 15- to 20-foot crag offering beginner climbs. It is not pictured.

**DIRECTIONS**

Many trails bisect Mount Marshall, but the shortest approach is to park at Skyline Drive mile marker 15.9. Follow the marked trail toward the summit of Mount Marshall. Within 0.4 mile you'll reach cliffs on the right. The highest cliffs are at the summit, but they are terraced, easy routes and are not pictured.

Reach the crag at Gravel Springs by parking at Gravel Springs Gap at Skyline Drive mile marker 17.7. Follow the marked trail toward Gravel Springs Hut, then follow the Appalachian Trail south for a quarter of a mile. Bushwhack down off the trail to the rocks.

Indian Run Rocks is located at Skyline Drive mile marker 43.

## MOUNT MARSHALL

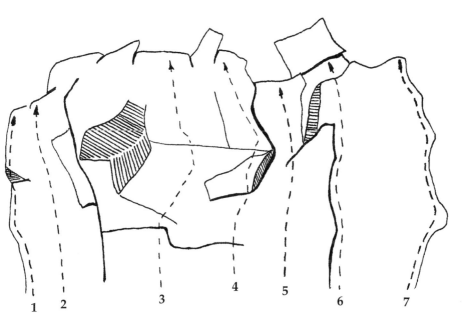

## ROUTE DESCRIPTIONS

### MOUNT MARSHALL

1. **5.9, 48 ft.**
   Climb the edge to the left of the face.

2. **5.7, 50 ft.**
   Climb the leaning ledge.

3. **5.13, 55 ft.**
   Climb the center of the overhang.

4. **5.11, 55 ft.**
   Climb the overhang to the right of the face.

5. **5.7, 50 ft.**
   Climb the smooth face just past climb 4.

## MOUNT MARSHALL

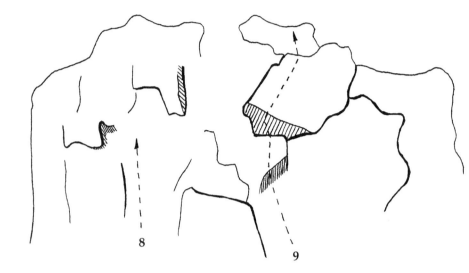

6  **5.6, 50 ft.**
   Climb the layback.

7  **5.5, 50 ft.**
   Climb the easy corner.

8  **5.3–5.7, 40 ft.**
   Just past the corner, climb the finger crack-covered wall.

9  **5.10-, 35 ft.**
   Climb over the two slight overhangs.

10 **5.8, 25 ft.**
   Climb the face on the right side of the walkdown.

11 **5.7, 25 ft.**
   Climb to the crack to the right of climb 10.

12 **5.5, 30 ft.**
   Start at the low overhang and continue up the flat wall.

## MOUNT MARSHALL

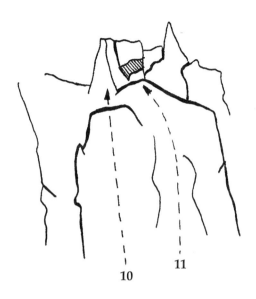

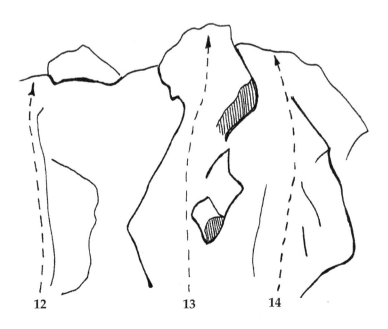

## MOUNT MARSHALL

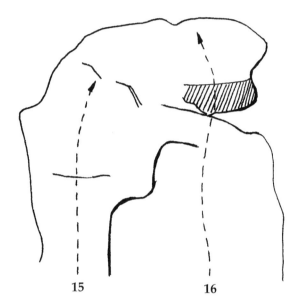

**13**  5.8, 30 ft.
Climb the center to the right of the block.

**14**  5.5, 32 ft.
Start on the far right of the block and climb the easy face.

**15**  5.5, 32 ft.
Climb the easy face around the corner from climb 14.

**16**  5.8, 35 ft.
Climb the overhang.

### NEARBY AREAS

See the other chapters on Shenandoah National Park for nearby climbing options.

### OTHER INFORMATION

Typical rules and regulations for Shenandoah National Park apply.

• CHAPTER 6 •

# Big Devils Stairs, Little Devils Stairs, Overall Run Falls

If you're looking for the long, leadable routes in this state, look no further than Big Devils Stairs. Situated in a deep canyon, these walls are about 120 feet tall. Sadly, the approach to this area is long because of a trail closure on the lower end.

Little Devils Stairs offers many good routes, some of which are leadable along a picturesque canyon. Expect some tough routes up to 65 feet.

Overall Run Falls has one good crag close to the Matthew's Arm campsites and occasionally has good ice or mixed routes over cascading falls.

### DIRECTIONS

Reach Big Devils Stairs from the Gravel Springs Gap Parking Area at Skyline Drive mile marker 17.7. Head toward the Gravel Springs Gap Hut and then follow the marked Bluff Trail 1.6 miles to Big Devils Stairs Trail. The trail no longer ends at Route 622. The tops of the cliffs are the overlook the trail passes over. There are also some lower crags in this area, some good bouldering, and a decent camp area by the overlooks. To reach the cliffs on the other side, hike upstream at the point where the trail crosses the stream. To return to the Skyline Drive, backtrack the way you came in. I don't recommend bushwhacking out because of some wet and loose 20-foot cliffs you'll have to pass over.

Little Devils Stairs can be reached from Skyline Drive mile marker 19.4. Park there and follow the marked trails to Fourway, then follow the Little Devils Stairs Trail. The trail is 2 miles long and ends at VA 614 (off VA 622). Parking and self-registration are available here. Do not park near private property or the "No Parking" signs. After climbing, the only way out is to either backtrack up the canyon or head up Keyser Run Fire Road. The fire road leads back to the top of the canyon.

Overall Run Falls can be reached from the Matthew's Arm camping area at Skyline Drive mile marker 22.2. In the summer, you can drive into the camping area; otherwise, you'll have to park and walk down. To reach the falls, start at Matthew's Arm camping area B by the sign "Tents only." Follow the marked trail 1 mile to Overall Run Trail. Bear left at the next concrete marker and go another 0.4 mile. The crag I have listed is closer, about 0.5 mile down the trail from camping area B.

## ROUTE DESCRIPTIONS

### BIG DEVILS STAIRS

The big leadable cliffs are under the overlooks you'll pass on the trail. They have long, deep cracks and many places for placing protection. The long route lines are obvious to the eye. This is a good area for practicing belaying on the wall, working out hauling techniques, and bivouacking. Here is a small sample of the many routes on the eastern canyon side. Directly upstream from the overlook is both a good camping spot and some nice bouldering problems. Directly below the overlook, you will find:

1   **Buttress 5.10, 120 ft.**
    Climb the buttress face and continue up the wall.

2   **5.10, 120 ft.**
    Follow the sickle-shaped edge.

Directly across from the overlook is a wall with great routes. Hike down to the bottom of the canyon and follow the stream up or rappel down out of the canyon and bushwhack over to the face. It is 60 to 70 feet tall. From downstream to upstream:

## BIG DEVILS STAIRS

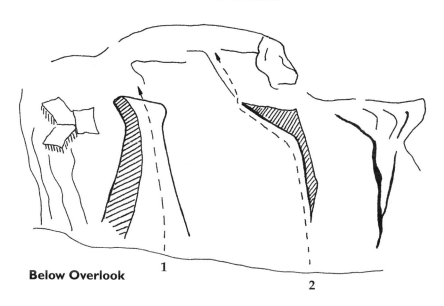

Below Overlook

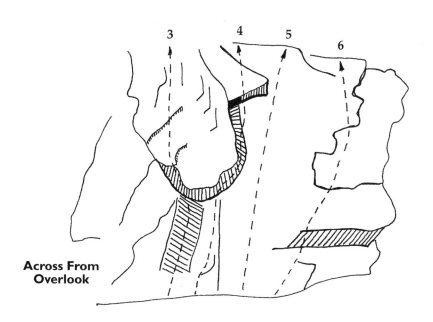

Across From Overlook

3   5.10, 70 ft.
    Climb up the depression and climb the overhang.
4   5.10, 70 ft.
    To the right of the bulging face, climb the edge.
5   5.10, 60 ft.
    Climb the face to the right of the bulging face.
6   5.9, 60 ft.
    On the upstream end of the face, climb the overhanging faces.

Also across the canyon are long ribbons of cliffs varying between 30 and 80 feet in height. In some spots, these ribbons are stacked two or three high. If you are hiking up the canyon from the very bottom,

**BIG DEVILS STAIRS**

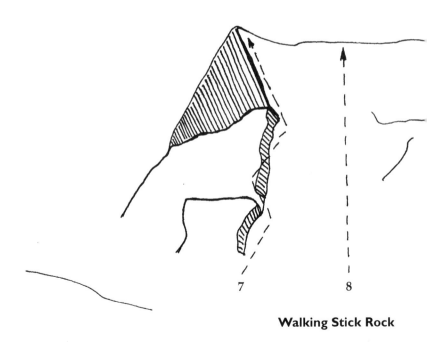

**Walking Stick Rock**

you will see Walking Stick Rock on the western side. Walking Stick Rock is named after the insects you'll find everywhere on warm summer days. It is a 40-foot crag. In addition to walking sticks, you will find loose rocks and hornets' nests.

7 **Zigzag Edge 5.7, 40 ft.**
Follow the edge formed by the overlapping faces.

8 **Walking Stick Face 5.9, 40 ft.**
Climb the face next to the overlapping faces.

9 **5.8, 40 ft.**
Climb the low overhang and finish on the face.

The cliff continues with some more routes.

**BIG DEVILS STAIRS**

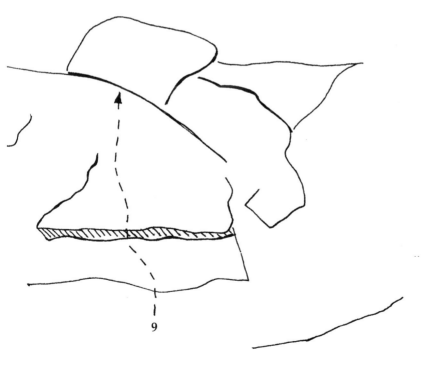

## LITTLE DEVILS STAIRS

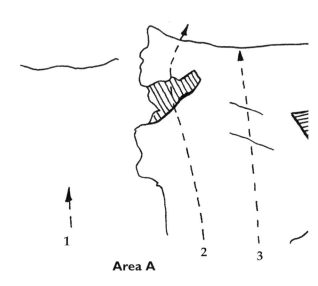

Area A

---

### LITTLE DEVILS STAIRS

#### Area A
This is a 25- to 30-foot west-facing cliff close to where the stream crosses the path.

1. **5.0–5.2, 25 ft.**
   Climb anywhere on the easy side of this face.

2. **5.9, 27 ft.**
   Climb the small overhang on the right side of the large crack.

3. **5.6, 28 ft.**
   Climb the face to the right of the overhang.

4. **5.6, 30 ft.**
   Climb over the leaning ledge.

5. **5.8, 30 ft.**
   Climb the overhanging edge.

6. **5.8, 30 ft.**
   Climb the face to the right of climb 5.

## LITTLE DEVILS STAIRS

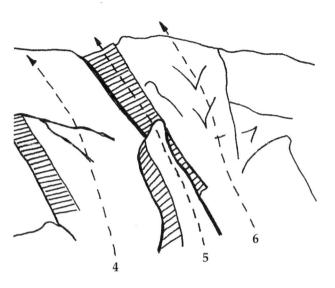

### Area B
Further downstream:

7   **5.10+, 30 ft.**
    Climb the leaning face. The rock here is loose, and the beginning moves are tough.

### Area C
Downstream from Area B, across the stream, the north side is mossy, overgrown, and between 25 and 45 feet tall. On the east side:

8   **5.10, 30 ft.**
    Climb the overhanging end.

9   **5.10, 30 ft**
    Climb the end over the bulging end.

10  **5.7, 26 ft**
    Take the easy route around the overhang.

11  **5.8, 30 ft.**
    Climb the face around the corner from the north side.

# LITTLE DEVILS STAIRS

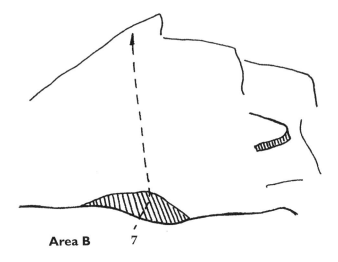

Area B    7

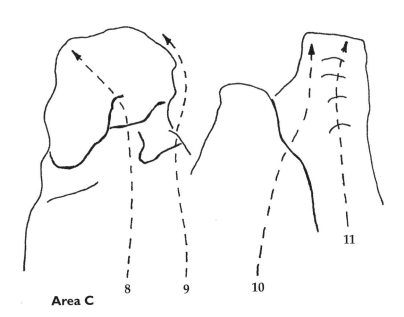

Area C    8    9    10    11

## Area D
Further downstream:

12. **The Bowl 5.5–5.7, 20 ft.**
    Climb anywhere on the bowl-shaped face.

13. **5.10, 25 ft.**
    Climb the overhanging end.

14. **5.8, 25 ft.**
    Climb the leaning face.

15. **5.10, 50 ft.**
    Climb over the overhanging blocks.

16. **5.9, 50 ft.**
    Climb the center of the leaning face.

17. **5.7, 50 ft.**
    Climb the corner.

**LITTLE DEVILS STAIRS**

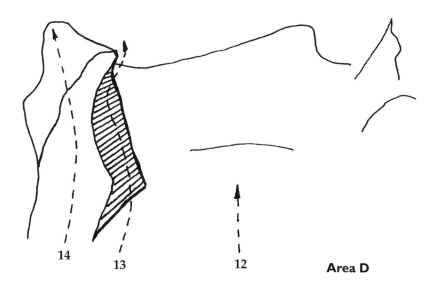

## LITTLE DEVILS STAIRS

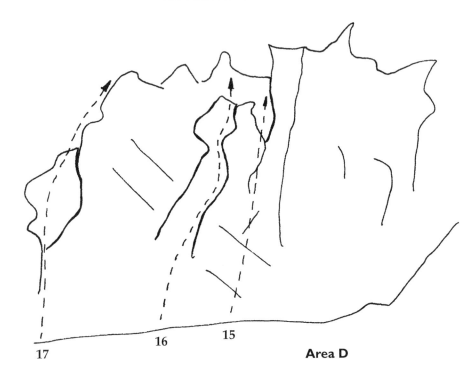

**Area E**
Located directly across the stream from Area D are these routes:

18  **5.7, 70 ft.**
    To the left of the caves, climb the face.

19  **5.10, 70 ft.**
    Between the two caves, climb the face.

20  **5.10, 70 ft.**
    Around the corner from the caves, climb the leaning face.

21  **5.6–5.9, 70 ft.**
    Several good routes to the left of climb 20.

## LITTLE DEVILS STAIRS

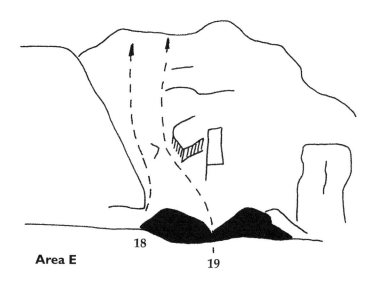

Area E
18
19

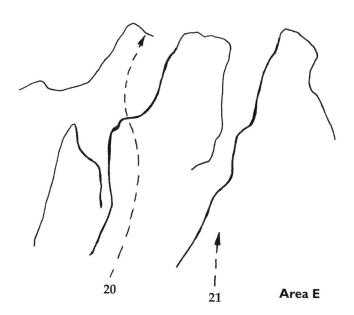

20
21
Area E

# LITTLE DEVILS STAIRS

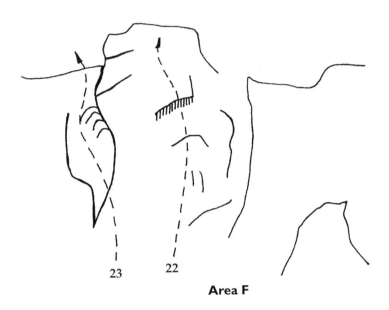

Area F

## Area F
Still further downstream where the path crosses the stream again:

22  5.10, 70 ft.
   Climb the face past the slight overhangs.

23  5.11, 67 ft.
   Climb the leaning face between the cracks.

Area F continues but is overgrown and smaller.

## Area G
This area is located directly across the stream from Area F and is not pictured. It is a 60-foot cliff that is often wet. It has some good cracks to the right of the mossy areas. One hundred yards down is a good route called the Thumb, 5.9, 35 ft. Climb the thumb-shaped pinnacle.

## OVERALL RUN FALLS

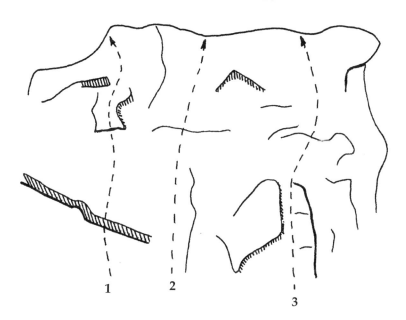

## OVERALL RUN FALLS

1  **5.8, 30 ft.**
   Climb past the outcroppings on the left end of the face.

2  **5.7, 30 ft.**
   Climb the center of the face.

3  **5.6, 30 ft.**
   Climb the right side of the cliff.

### NEARBY AREAS

See the other chapters on Shenandoah National Park for more climbing options.

## OTHER INFORMATION

You can camp around the Appalachian Trail near but not in view of the Gravel Springs Hut. Good camping is available at the Matthew's Arm campsite. There is also a good camp area off the Big Devils Stairs trail near some 30-foot boulders. See Appendix B for more information on Shenandoah National Park rules and regulations. Remember to get a backcountry permit for camping.

• CHAPTER 7 •

# Marys Rock, The Pinnacles

Marys Rock contains six small cliffs with heights up to 40 feet. Northern Virginia climbers will recognize a similarity between Carderock in Maryland and Marys Rock—short routes with some difficult problems. Marys Rock is also a fine area for bouldering.

The Pinnacles is a tiny bouldering area near Marys Rock. Marys Rock and other cliffs along Skyline Drive make a far better climbing choice than The Pinnacles.

## DIRECTIONS

Marys Rock is located at Skyline Drive mile marker 31.5. Park in the Thornton Gap Panorama parking area. Follow the Marys Rock Trail up 1.7 miles to a mile marker. (Get your partner to carry the rope up.) The areas are arranged as follows: To reach Area B or the tops of C and D, follow the trail 0.1 mile to the summit of Marys Rock. To reach Area F or the base of C and D, turn left and follow the trail away from the summit about 50 yards. To reach Areas E and F, descend from either path.

## MARYS ROCK CLIMBING AREAS

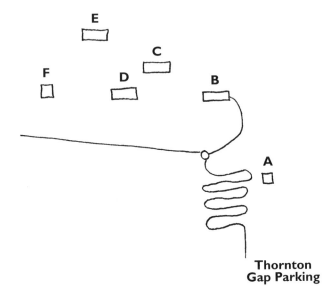

## ROUTE DESCRIPTIONS

### AREA A

Four or five great bouldering problems exist along the path on the way from Thornton Gap to the summit of Marys Rock. Here's a good chance to warm up and give your partner with the rope a rest. The boulders are shown in the order that you'll come to them.

1. **5.7, 20 ft.**
   Climb the leaning smooth face.

2. **5.10, 20 ft.**
   Climb the overhanging block.

3. **The Table 5.11, 12 ft.**
   Climb the low ceiling.

## MARYS ROCK

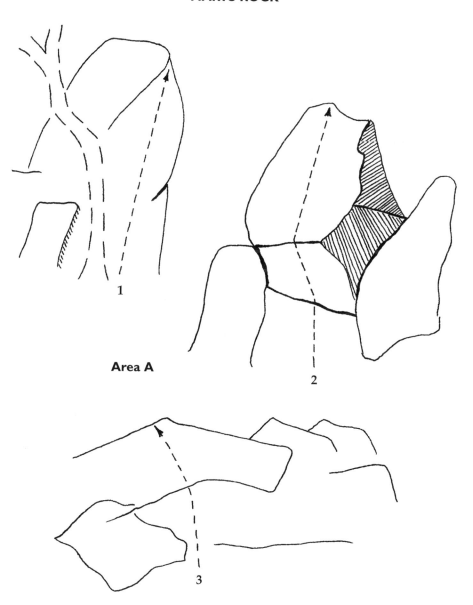

Area A

## MARYS ROCK

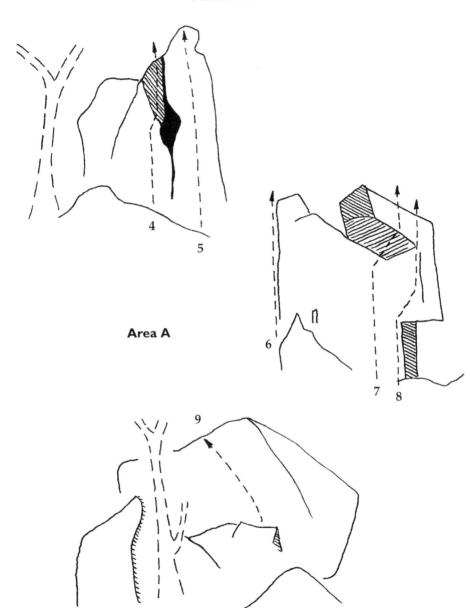

Area A

4   **5.5, 25 ft.**
    Chimney up to a small crack and follow the crack.

5   **5.9, 30 ft.**
    Climb the tough face.

Climbs 6–8 are on the north side of climbs 4 and 5. Look for the Appalachian Trail blaze marks on the face.

6   **5.7, 30 ft.**
    Climb the corner.

7   **5.10-, 30 ft.**
    Climb smooth face and go over the 2-foot overhang.

8   **5.5, 28 ft.**
    Climb the edge to the crack and follow the crack.

9   **5.10+, 20 ft.**
    Climb the leaning face.

## AREA B

There is a 50-foot cliff directly below the summit of Marys Rock, usable mostly for beginners and bouldering. Due to the low angle, only the top 20 to 25 feet of this cliff are vertical. The easiest descent, besides rappelling, is a chimney. Go down the chimney and face south. Pass under the ledge. Beginner's face has a southeast face. There is good bouldering on the other end of the descent chimney.

10  **Beginner's cracks 5.3, 20 ft.**
    Climb to the ledge and climb either crack.

11  **Beginner's face 5.3–5.4, 22 ft.**
    Climb the center face.

12  **Leaning crack 5.3, 20 ft.**
    Climb the crack.

13  **5.6, 25 ft.**
    Climb the smooth face to a mild overhang.

## MARYS ROCK

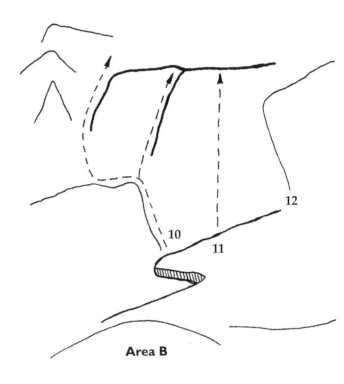

Area B

## AREAS C AND D

There are various cliff faces with cracks of all widths and sizes. For east faces:

14   **5.5, 20 ft.**
Climb the smooth face to the right of the V-shaped rock.

15   **5.3, 24 ft.**
As above, but jam the crack.

16   **5.5, 20 ft.**
Climb up the block and traverse over to the top of jam crack.

## MARYS ROCK

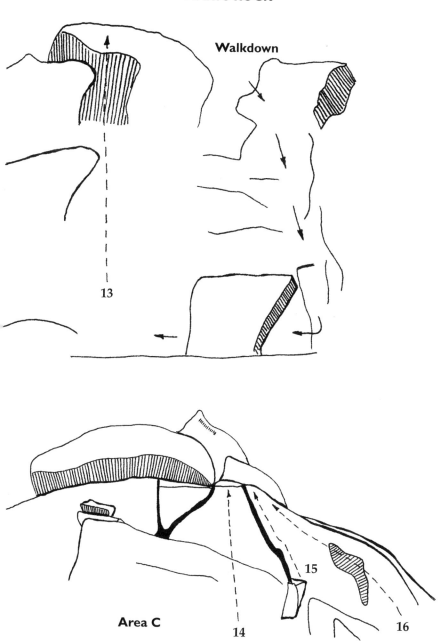

## MARYS ROCK

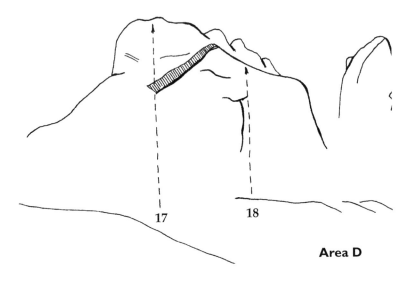

Area D

17  **5.6, 40 ft.**
    Climb the smooth face.

18  **5.6, 30 ft.**
    Climb past the thin crack to the top ledge.

19  **5.4, 30 ft.**
    Climb the crack.

20  **5.5, 35 ft.**
    Climb the layback.

21  **5.8, 40 ft.**
    Climb the smooth face.

22  **5.5, 40 ft.**
    Climb using layback or jamming techniques.

23  **5.8, 40 ft.**
    Climb the face anywhere to the right of the jam crack.

24  **5.4, 25 ft.**
    Climb the easy face.

## MARYS ROCK

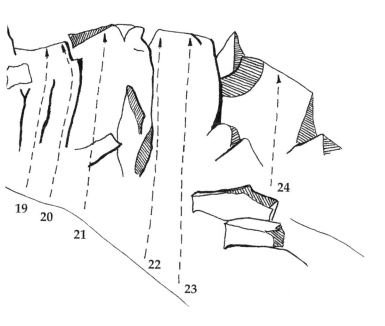

## AREA E

There are some nice routes on these lower ridges, and up to 30-foot heights on east faces.

25  **5.6, 20 ft.**
    Climb the off-width crack. Variation: Climb the crack to the 9-foot overhang.

26  **5.9, 30 ft.**
    Climb the smooth face to the right of the off-width crack.

27  **5.6, 30 ft.**
    Climb the crack to the microledge and bear left around the overhanging block. Variation: 5.10; climb the overhang just past the crack.

## MARYS ROCK

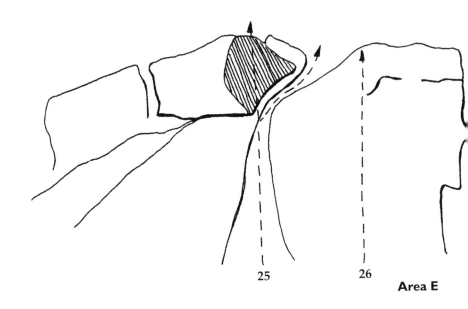

**Area E**

28  **Chimney 5.3, 30 ft.**
At the right of the overhanging block, climb the chimney between the faces.

29  **5.5, 30 ft.**
Climb the right corner face of the chimney.

30  **5.6, 30 ft.**
Layback the crack.

31  **5.7, 28 ft.**
Climb the smooth face to the right of the crack.

32  **5.9, 26 ft.**
As above, but stay farther to right.

33  **5.8, 22 ft.**
Located around the corner from climbs 31 and 32. Climb the corner.

## MARYS ROCK

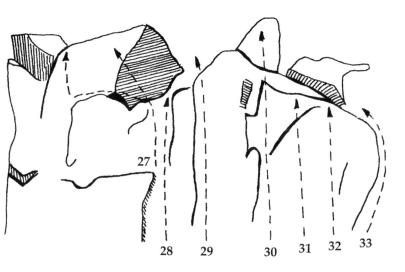

### AREA F

This is a small block with good overhang problems. Directly in front of this cliff is an 8-foot altar.

34  **Big-Budget Sacrifice 5.11+, 25 ft.**
    Starting on the left thin crack, climb the overhang.

35  **B-Movie Sacrifice 5.10+, 25 ft.**
    Starting on the right thin crack, stay to the right of the bulge.

36  **Musical Sacrifice 5.6, 15 ft.**
    Climb the far right crack and avoid the overhang to the right.

### NEARBY AREAS

See the other chapters on Shenandoah National Park for more climbing options.

The Pinnacles offer average bouldering. Don't go out of your way for these rocks. Park at the Jewel Hollow Overlook and walk 50 feet

## MARYS ROCK

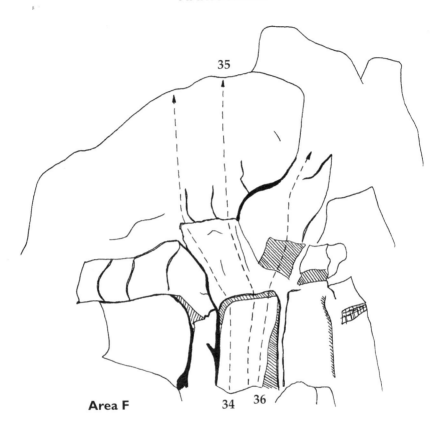

Area F

to the Appalachian Trail. Go toward The Pinnacles picnic area. The rocks are 25 to 30 feet tall with one good overhang.

Avoid Betty's Rock. This low-angle boulder has no value to climbers.

### OTHER INFORMATION

See Appendix B for more information on Shenandoah National Park and Skyline Drive. Camping is free, but you must have a permit. Get one from the rangers at the Thornton Gap entrance. No camping is allowed in sight of the trail, and no fires are permitted. Filter your water. Beware of skunks, bears, and ticks.

· CHAPTER 8 ·

# Little Stony Man Cliffs, Crescent Rocks

Shenandoah National Park calls this a great place for watching sunsets. It may be, but it's a better place for climbing. I've even done some August night climbing here under the shooting stars. Discovered by only a few, Little Stony Man Cliffs is a great area for climbing. It has everything except the crowds. It has spots to place protection (traditional please), cracks, overhangs, and off-widths; routes range from beginner's up through the grades. At their tallest, these greenstone cliffs reach 100 feet.

Crescent Rocks, another nearby but smaller area, also has routes reaching 100 feet in height. Crescent Rocks has much loose rock and one tremendous overhang. More routes are possible than are listed, so feel free to explore.

### DIRECTIONS

Reach Little Stony Man Cliffs by parking at the Little Stony Man Parking Area at Skyline Drive mile marker 39.1. Head up the trail toward the summit. In 0.4 mile, you will reach a milepost. Stay to your right, toward Furnace Springs, for the quickest approach to the bottom of the cliffs. Alternatively, you can follow the marked trail up 0.9 mile to the top of Little Stony Man Cliffs. Passing over the cliff tops will bring you to several good walkdown areas or points for attaching a rappel. You can also continue 0.4 mile to the summit. There are also some good climbs on the summit of Stony Man

Mountain (these are not pictured). The Little Stony Man Cliffs climbs are pictured as you come across them.

Reach Crescent Rocks by parking at the Crescent Rocks Overlook and going south down the trail for about 100 yards. This brings you to the top of the cliffs. Go to the north end of the cliffs for the easiest walkdown.

## ROUTE DESCRIPTIONS

### LITTLE STONY MAN CLIFFS

The cliff starts out easy but has some good bouldering spots. In front of this area is a good leaning boulder. There is also a crag below the leaning boulder. At the end of this crag is a large blocky overhang with several routes.

1  40 ft.
   Good bouldering.

### LITTLE STONY MAN CLIFFS

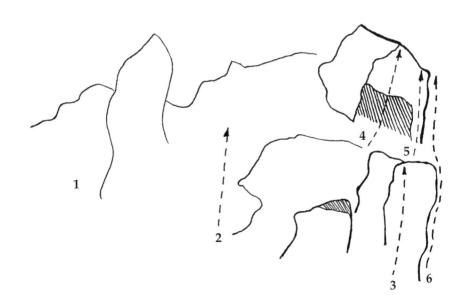

2   **5.2–5.3, 40 ft.**
    Blocky and terraced face.

3   **5.6, 30 ft.**
    On the lower section, climb the face.

4   **5.10, 30 ft.**
    On the upper section, climb the large blocky overhang.

5   **5.6, 30 ft.**
    Climb the upper face to the right of the overhang.

6   **5.7, 30 ft.**
    Around the corner from climb 5, climb the face.

7   **5.7, 60 ft.**
    To the right of the separation, climb the edge.

8   **5.6, 60 ft.**
    Climb the slight overhang.

## LITTLE STONY MAN CLIFFS

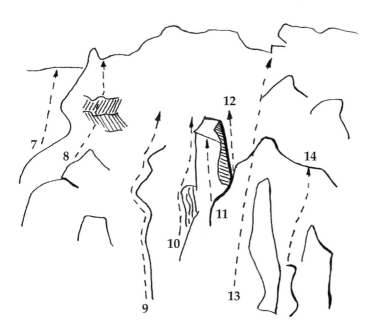

## LITTLE STONY MAN CLIFFS

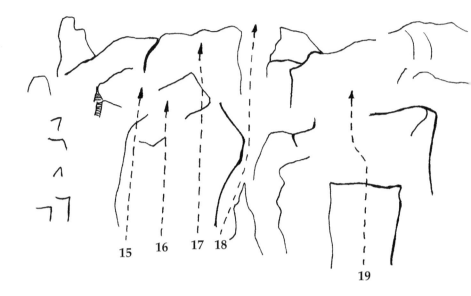

9  **5.7, 50 ft**
   Follow the crack.

10 **5.4, 50 ft.**
   On the left side of the detached block, climb the face.

11 **5.9, 50 ft.**
   In the center of the detached block, climb the face.

12 **5.5, 50 ft.**
   On the right side of the detached block, climb the face.

13 **5.4, 50 ft.**
   Follow the easy route up through the terraced edges.

14 **5.9, 50 ft.**
   Climb the leaning face.

15 **5.6, 60 ft.**
   Follow the crack.

## LITTLE STONY MAN CLIFFS

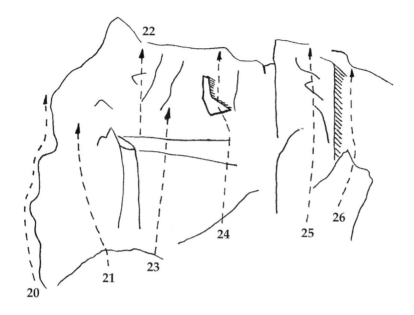

16  **5.8, 60 ft.**
    Climb the leaning face.

17  **5.10, 60 ft.**
    Climb the face, avoiding the cracks.

18  **5.4, 70 ft.**
    Climb the long chimney.

19  **5.3–5.5, 70 ft.**
    Easy crack-filled and blocky wall; excellent for practicing gear placements, especially micronuts.

20  **5.3, 60 ft.**
    Climb the easy crack.

21  **5.10, 50 ft.**
    Difficult start, then follow the leaning face.

## LITTLE STONY MAN CLIFFS

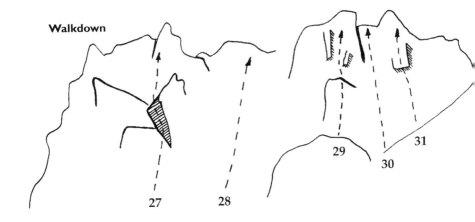

22  **5.8, 50 ft.**
    Starting below the shrub-covered terrace, climb the face.

23  **5.7, 50 ft.**
    Make your way up the terraces and climb the face above.

24  **5.8, 50 ft.**
    Climb the face by the detached block.

25  **5.4, 50 ft.**
    Climb the easy face.

26  **5.5, 50 ft.**
    To the right of the separating block, climb the face.

At this point, you will arrive at a walkdown. Past the walkdown:

27  **5.5, 80 ft.**
    To the left of the overhanging block, climb the face.

28  **5.2–5.3, 80 ft.**
    Climb anywhere on this blocky, terraced face.

29  **5.8, 100 ft.**
    Climb the face behind the detached boulder.

**30  5.5, 100 ft.**
Follow the 100-foot hand crack or try a long layback.

**31  5.4, 100 ft.**
Climb the easy face.

There are more climbs if you continue up this path, including some rock on the summit.

## CRESCENT ROCKS

I've listed only two of the many possible routes in this area. Although it's not the best area, it does have one of the shortest approaches possible.

**1  Overhang Wall 5.10, 55 ft.**
Climb the sharply leaning face.

On the main wall:

**2  5.7–5.9, 100 ft.**
Climb the face on the southern side of Overhang Wall.

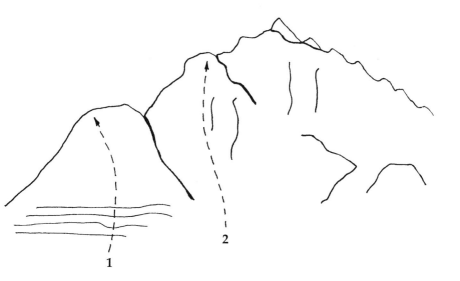

**CRESCENT ROCKS**

## NEARBY AREAS

There are many climbing areas nearby in Shenandoah National Park (see other chapters).

## OTHER INFORMATION

See Appendix B for information regarding rules, regulations, and camping areas in Shenandoah National Park.

• CHAPTER 9 •

# White Oak Canyon Cliffs

The cliffs along the White Oak Canyon Trail are Virginia's greatest undeveloped rock climbing area. The trail itself is pleasant, passing by six waterfalls, the highest being 86 feet. Climbers will find a good variety of routes up to 80 feet. The canyon also is Virginia's best (and almost only) area for ice climbing. Good ice routes appear almost every winter. Look for wet autumns and winters, along with low temperatures. If you are interested in the ice routes, bring short screws, some ice pitons, and medium-sized chocks.

## DIRECTIONS

White Oak Canyon is located on Skyline Drive at mile marker 42.6. If this parking lot is full, as it usually is on weekends, drive south and turn left just past mile marker 43 onto a dirt road. At either parking area, follow the trail markers. The furthest climbs listed here are less than 3 miles from the trail, but you'll have to go only about three-quarters of a mile to reach some challenging climbs. Despite the sign, the trail is relatively easy. When Shenandoah National Park calls the trail strenuous, it usually means that the rangers haven't gotten around to building a footbridge over every creek.

## Area A

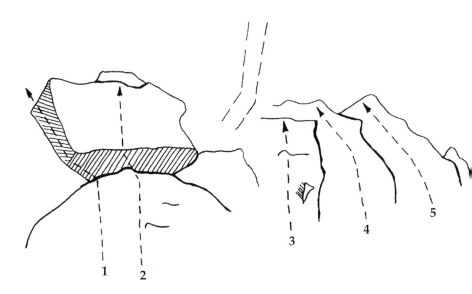

## ROUTE DESCRIPTIONS

### AREA A

After the first bridge, cross the creek and approach the northwest-facing boulder.

1 **5.12, 18 ft.**
 Climb the face and the overhanging block.

2 **5.10, 20 ft.**
 Climb the face and the 8-foot overhang.

3 **5.5, 20 ft.**
 Climb the easy face to the right of the overhanging block.

4 **5.1, 25 ft.**
 Climb the middle of the easy face.

5 **5.2, 25 ft.**
 Climb the right face.

Climbs 6 to 10 are on a northwest-facing cliff behind the overhanging boulder.

6   **5.12, 20 ft.**
    Climb the leaning face.

7   **5.10, 20 ft.**
    Climb the crack on the leaning face.

8   **5.11, 20 ft.**
    Climb the leaning face to the right of the crack.

9   **5.12, 20 ft.**
    Climb the leaning face by the horizontal tree.

10  **5.4, 16 ft.**
    Layback the crack to the right of the horizontal tree.

## AREA B

There is good bouldering rock along the trail. From the trail, you can see the southwest face, but the routes are on the east and the northwest. Bring long webbing for protection.

### East Face

11  **5.10, 20 ft.**
    Climb the leaning face.

12  **5.10, 20 ft.**
    Climb the right corner of the leaning face.

### Northwest Face

13  **5.11, 24 ft.**
    Climb the face to the left of the bulge.

14  **5.12, 24 ft.**
    Climb the center of the smooth face.

15  **5.9, 24 ft.**
    Climb the right side of the face past the slight overhang.

## Area A

## Area B

**East Face**

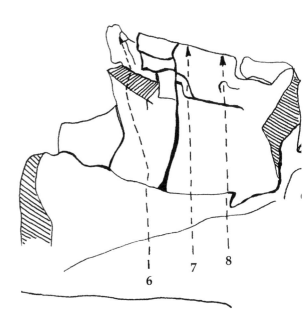

White Oak Canyon Cliffs • 101

**Area A**

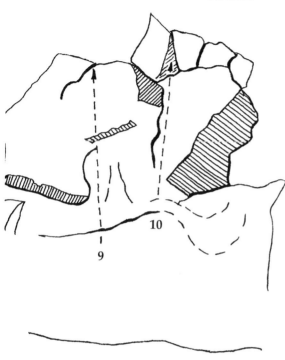

**Area B**

**Northwest Face**

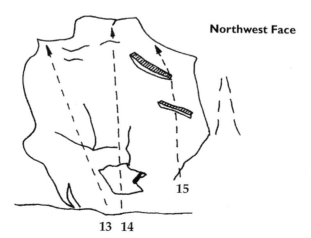

## AREA C

Reach northwest-facing Area C by bushwhacking down from Area A or by crossing the creek around Area B.

**16**  **5.3, 30 ft.**
Easy scramble up to a large ledge.

**17**  **UTOH 5.9, 25 ft.**
On upper terrace, climb the leaning face.

**18**  **Cracked Edge 5.8, 20 ft.**
On upper terrace, climb the right edge.

**19**  **5.7, 15 ft.**
On the west side of the upper terrace, climb the center of the face.

**20**  **5.6, 25 ft.**
Climb the easy face over small terraces.

**21**  **5.1, 25 ft.**
Climb the easy face.

**22**  **5.5, 22 ft.**
Climb the face just to the right of the edge.

**23**  **5.6, 12 ft.**
Climb the short leaning slab.

**24**  **5.7, 15 ft.**
Follow the crack to the blank face.

**25**  **5.5, 15 ft.**
Climb the edge.

**26**  **5.4, 25 ft.**
Climb the easy face to a small outcrop.

**27**  **5.6, 25 ft.**
Follow the crack.

**28**  **5.9, 20 ft.**
Climb the leaning face.

White Oak Canyon Cliffs • 103

## Area C

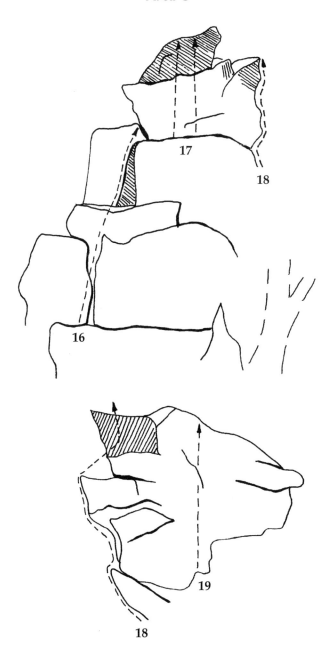

## Area C

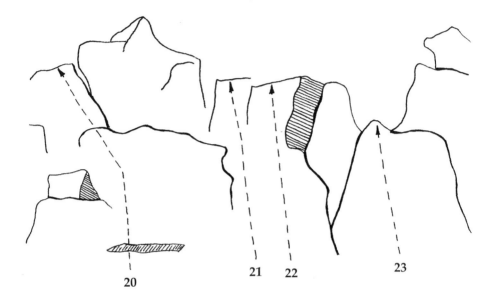

29   **5.9, 20 ft.**
    Climb the leaning face and pull the overhang. Variation: 5.6, 20 ft. Pass to the right and avoid the overhang.

30   **5.4, 20 ft.**
    Climb the easy face to the right of the overhang.

31   **5.3, 20 ft.**
    Follow the crack up.

32   **5.9, 20 ft.**
    Climb the smooth leaning face.

33   **5.7, 20 ft.**
    Follow the edge to the wide crack.

34   **5.8, 20 ft.**
    Climb the face leaning away from the large ledge.

## Area C

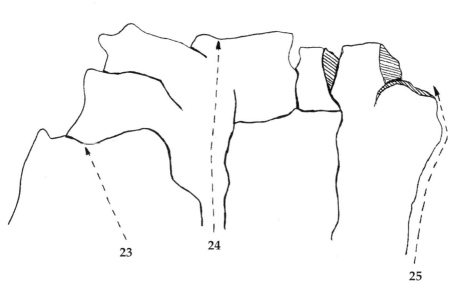

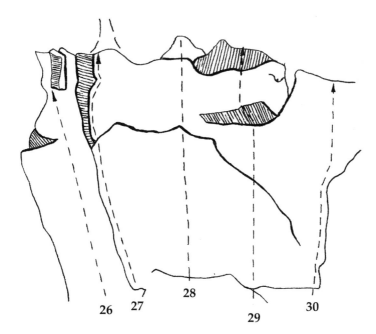

## Area C

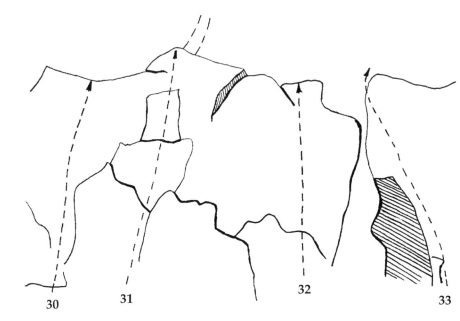

35 **5.6, 20 ft.**
Follow the crack to the right of climb 34.

36 **Do-good 5.7, 20 ft.**
Follow the tough crack.

37 **Do-gooder 5.10, 20 ft.**
Climb the smooth leaning face.

38 **Do-gooder Sidekick 5.6, 20 ft.**
Climb the edge of the west side.

39 **5.1, 20 ft.**
Climb the easy corner.

40 **Did Better 5.9, 18 ft.**
Climb the leaning slab.

# Area C

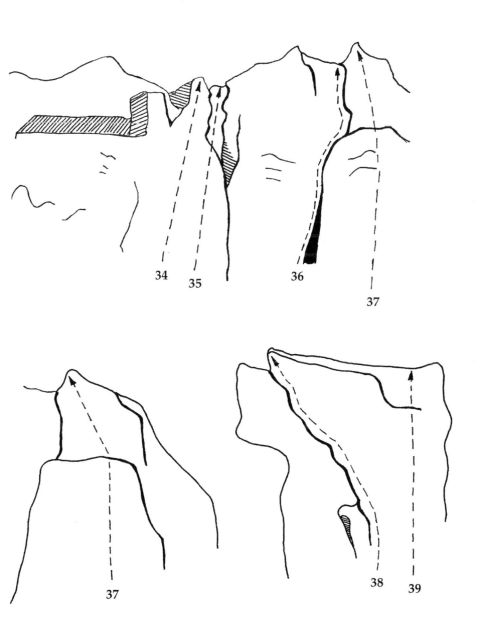

## Area C

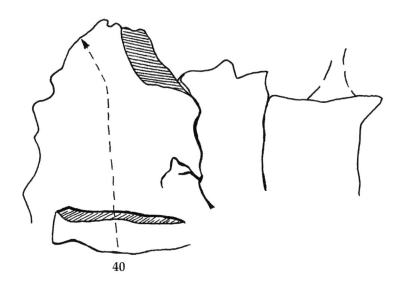

40

## AREA D

This area is also located across the creek. Bushwhack downstream from Area C or cross the creek by Area E.

### Southwest Face

41  5.6, 25 ft.
    Climb the flaky face.

42  5.6, 25 ft.
    Climb the edge of the detached flake.

43  5.7, 25 ft.
    Climb the smooth face to the right of the detached flake.

44  5.6, 25 ft.
    Climb the face to the right of the smooth face.

### North Cliff

45  5.7, 18 ft.
    Climb the face between the two trees.

# White Oak Canyon Cliffs • 109

## Area D

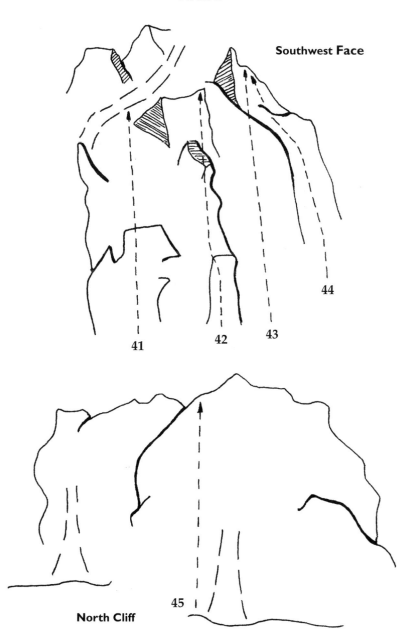

## Area D

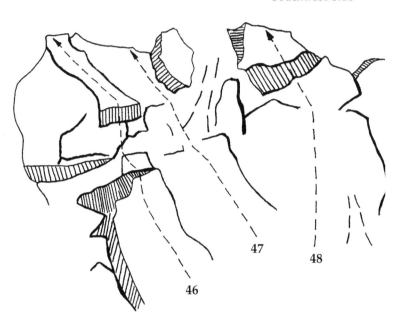

## Southwest Side

46 **5.7, 25 ft.**
Climb the face and the small overhang.

47 **5.6, 25 ft.**
Climb the face just to the left of the large outcropping.

48 **5.9, 30 ft.**
Climb the slab to the steep overhang.

49 **5.9, 25 ft.**
Climb the leaning face.

50 **5.9, 25 ft.**
Climb the leaning face to the overhanging block.

## Area D

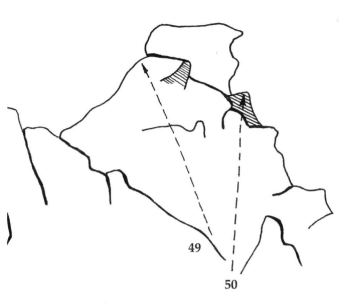

## West Face

**51  5.2, 40 ft.**
Climb the easy face.

**52  5.5, 50 ft.**
Climb the easy edge to the easy face.

**53  5.4, 52 ft.**
Climb the off-width chimney.

**54  5.11, 60 ft.**
Climb the difficult face on the left of the outcropping.

**55  The Tower 5.10, 60 ft.**
Climb the difficult face to the leaning overhang.

## Area D

**West Face**

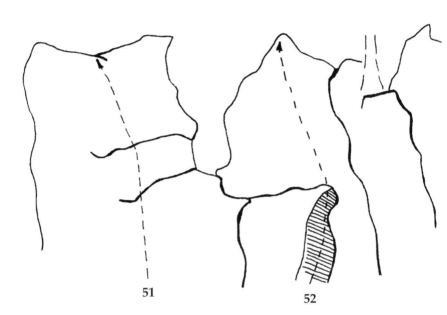

56   **5.9, 60 ft.**
As above, but avoid the leaning overhang.

57   **5.7, 60 ft.**
Climb the edge to the right of The Tower.

58   **Shycrack 5.9, 60 ft.**
A leadable crack.

59   **5.7, 60 ft.**
Good crack for those learning to lead.

## Area D

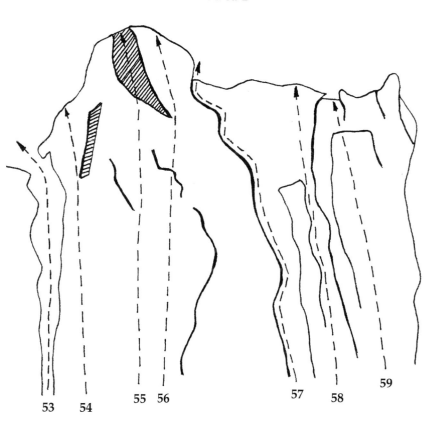

60  **5.5, 40 ft.**
   Follow the obvious route through the flakes.

From here on, the cliff continues but is a series of Grade IV climbs and damp walls with some fair beginner's routes. The cliff and drawings pick up directly over the creek.

61  **5.5, 70 ft.**
   Climb anywhere to the left of the large corner.

62  **5.6, 70 ft.**
   Climb the large corner.

## Area D

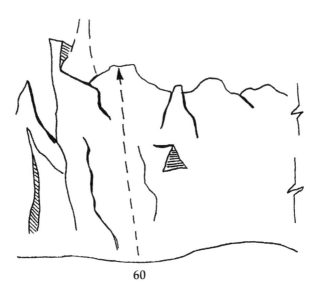

60

63   **5.9, 78 ft.**
   Climb the smooth face to the leaning blocks.

64   **5.8, 65 ft.**
   Climb the face to the highest point to the right of the leaning block.

   The cliff continues but is not pictured. It is usually damp in this area and is a mixture of Grade IV and beginner's routes. As you head back to the river from this point, you'll come across a 10- to 15-foot leaning block that has a few good boulder routes (not pictured).

## AREA E

There are no good climbs on this rock, but bushwhack behind it 25 yards for a boulderer's paradise.

## Area D

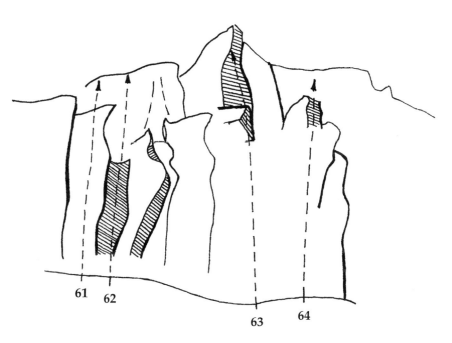

## Area E

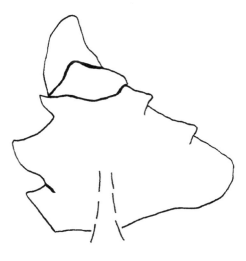

## Area F

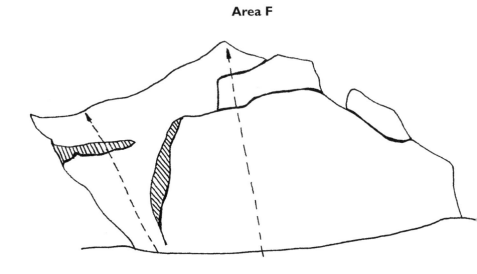

### AREA F

There is a 20-foot southwest-facing boulder with two short 5.7 routes.

### AREA G

There are east-facing cliffs at the base of the first falls.

65  **The Spray 5.7, 50 ft.**
    At the uppermost end of the base of the first falls, climb the face to the left of the outcropping.

66  **Mist Crack 5.9, 50 ft.**
    Climb the difficult crack.

67  **5.9, 60 ft.**
    Climb the large overhang.

68  **5.10, 60 ft.**
    Climb the leaning face.

69  **5.8, 60 ft.**
    Climb the face to the right of the leaning face.

70  **5.6, 60 ft.**
Climb the easy face. The occasional ice runnels here create some interesting mixed routes. A great practice area for aspiring ice climbers.

71  **5.8, 65 ft.**
Climb the overhang to the easier face.

72  **5.9, 65 ft.**
Climb the smooth edge.

73  **5.9, 65 ft.**
Climb the smooth face to the right of the large edge.

74  **5.9, 68 ft.**
Stay to the left of the leaning face.

75  **5.10, 70 ft.**
Climb the leaning face; stay to the right.

76  **5.5, 75 ft.**
Climb the crack.

77  **5.9, 80 ft.**
Climb the face; stay away from the cracks.

78  **5.7, 80 ft.**
Follow the leadable crack.

79  **5.6, 80 ft.**
Climb the easy face to the crack between the slabs.

80  **5.12, 80 ft.**
Climb the leaning face.

81  **5.10, 80 ft.**
Follow the leaning right edge.

82  **5.10, 85 ft.**
Climb the leaning face.

83  **5.10, 80 ft.**
After a difficult start, follow the leaning edge.

## Area G

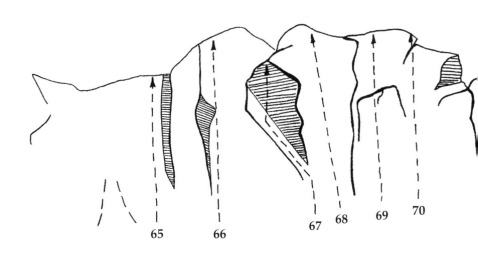

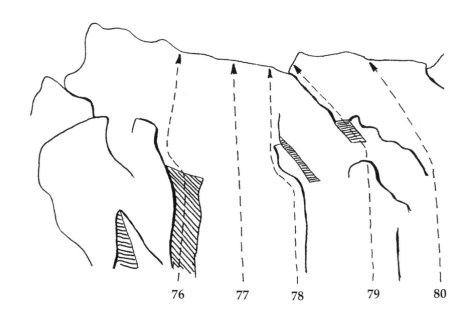

White Oak Canyon Cliffs • 119

## Area G

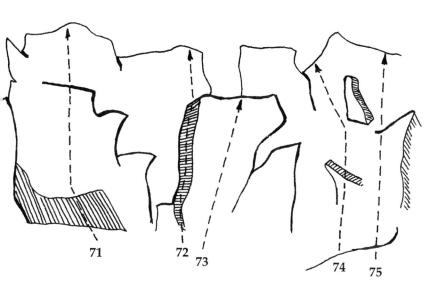
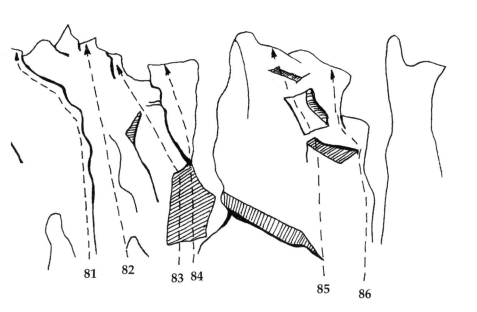

84  **5.10, 80 ft.**
   Same start as climb 83, but then follow the crack.

85  **5.10, 85 ft.**
   Climb the smooth leaning face over the 3-foot overhang.

86  **5.4, 85 ft.**
   Climb the crack, going around the overhang and up. Variation: Chimney up to the crack.

87  **5.2, 80 ft.**
   Climb the easy face anywhere.

From this point, the cliff is Grade IV. The climbs resume at a height of 50 feet.

88  **5.7, 50 ft.**
   Follow the easy ledges.

89  **5.9, 50 ft.**
   Avoiding edges and cracks, climb the face.

**Area G**

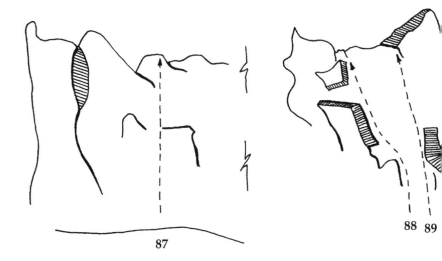

90  **5.6, 35 ft.**
    Climb the outcropping edge.

91  **5.3, 40 ft.**
    Climb the easy face to the right of the outcrop.

92  **The Next One 5.9, 60 ft.**
    Climb the leaning face.

93  **No Bars Hold 5.10, 60 ft.**
    Climb the leaning face.

94  **5.10, 60 ft.**
    Climb the end of the leaning overhang.

95  **Look Ma, Climbing 5.10, 60 ft.**
    Climb the leaning face beside the step. Stay to the left of the overhang or go through the center of it.

**Area G**

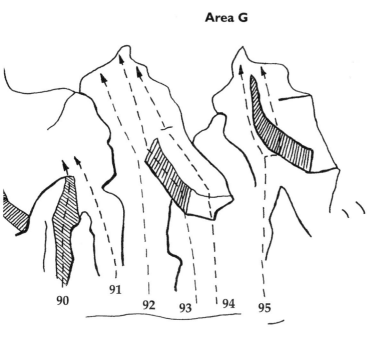

## Area H

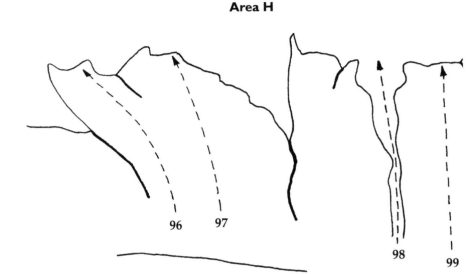

### AREA H

There are good south-facing cliffs along the path, but they are damp and dirty.

- 96 **5.9, 30 ft.**
  Climb the leaning face.

- 97 **5.8, 30 ft.**
  Climb the face.

- 98 **Jam Crack 5.3, 40 ft.**
  Follow the wide crack.

- 99 **Dirt Face 5.4, 40 ft.**
  Climb the dirty wall.

- 100 **No More Chalk 5.4–5.7, 40 ft.**
  Climb anywhere on the 60-foot-wide face or traverse it. Beware: it is usually damp.

- 101 **5.8, 25 ft.**
  Climb the leaning face and overhang.

## Area H

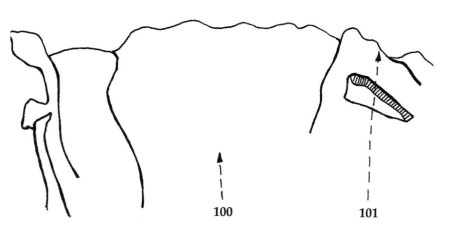

## AREA I

This area is located on the river side of the path.

### North Side

102  **5.8, 18 ft.**
     Climb the sharply overhanging face.

### Southeast Side

103  **5.8, 20 ft.**
     Traverse upward to the right.

   For the really daring:

104  **Wetfront, Wetback 5.12+, 20 ft.**
     At river level, climb the 15-foot ceiling.

## Area I

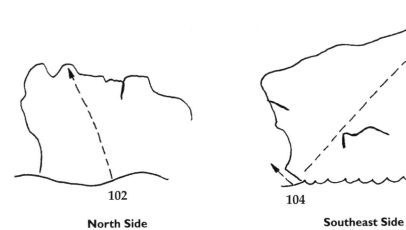

North Side

Southeast Side

## Area J

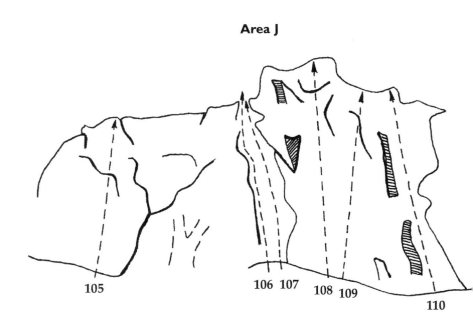

## AREA J

There is a 40-foot cliff along the trail.

**105**  **5.1, 25 ft.**
Climb the easy face.

**106**  **5.9, 30 ft.**
Climb the smooth inner face.

**107**  **5.4, 30 ft.**
Climb the wide chimney.

**108**  **5.10, 40 ft.**
Climb the leaning face.

**109**  **5.9, 38 ft.**
Climb the center of the leaning face.

**110**  **5.9, 38 ft.**
Climb the smooth right end.

**111**  **5.7, 30 ft.**
Directly around the corner from climb 110, climb anywhere on the wall.

**Area J**

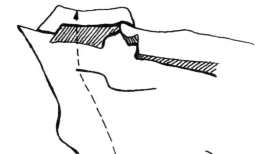

## Area K

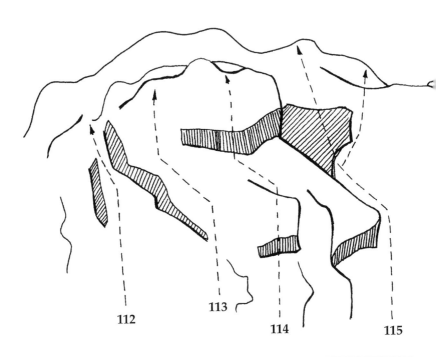

### AREA K

This area is 30 yards down the trail, south facing.

112  5.8, 50 ft.
Stay to the right of the overhang.

113  5.9, 55 ft.
Climb the face to the right of the overhang.

114  5.10, 55 ft.
Climb through the center of the overhangs.

115  5.9, 55 ft.
To the right of the large overhangs, climb the face and the big outcrop. Variation: 5.4; avoid the outcrop and head right.

## Area K

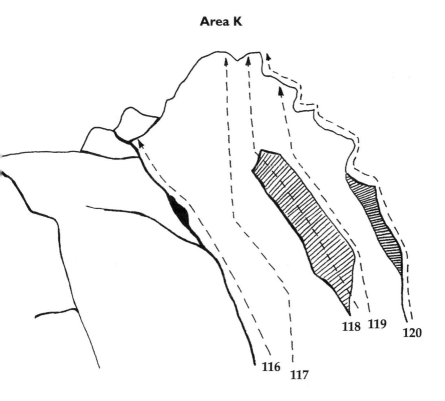

**116** 5.5, 50 ft.
Follow the large crack. Variation: 5.2; follow the left split.

**117** 5.9, 55 ft.
Climb the face to the left of the diagonal overhang.

**118** 5.10, 55 ft.
Climb the diagonal overhang.

**119** 5.9, 55 ft.
Stay to the right of the diagonal.

**120** 5.7, 55 ft.
Follow the corner.

From here, go east 25 yards to a good bouldering area or 25 feet south to a 10-foot roof problem (not pictured).

## AREA L

Hardstart Rock is a southwest-facing cliff along the trail next to a poison ivy sign. This 20-foot cliff lives up to its name.

**121 Hardstart 5.9, 20 ft.**
On the left end, climb the face starting anywhere in the overhang.

**122 Easystart 5.7, 20 ft.**
Climb the left face; avoid the overhang.

**123 5.3, 20 ft.**
Easy after the first move; follow the edge of either flake.

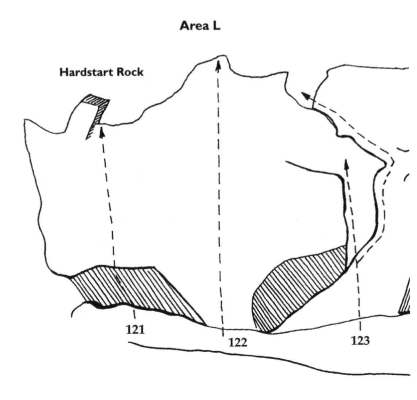

Area L

**124  TicTacToe 5.9, 20 ft.**
Climb the leaning face through the scar shaped like a tic-tac-toe board.

**125  5.8, 20 ft.**
Climb the leaning face.

**126  5.9, 20 ft.**
Climb the 8-foot ceiling and the leaning face.

**127  5.10, 20 ft.**
Climb the 15-foot ceiling and the leaning face.

Around the corner from climb 126 is a 20-foot wall with some 5.5 routes (not pictured).

**Area L**

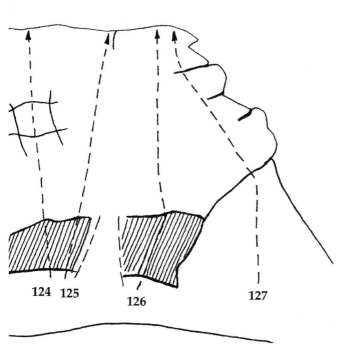

## Area M

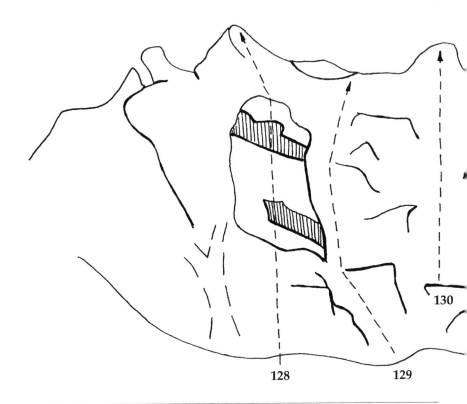

### AREA M

The south-facing crag is off the trail, just past Hardstart Rock.

**128** **5.9, 50 ft.**
Climb the bulging overhangs.

**129** **5.3, 50 ft.**
Climb anywhere to the right of climb 128.

**130** **5.4, 55 ft.**
Climb the center face.

**131** **5.6, 60 ft.**
Follow the crack by the large flake.

## Area M

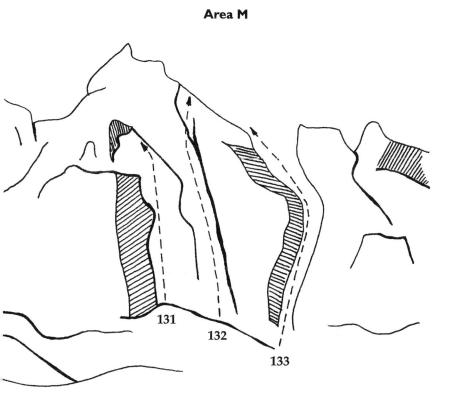

**132  5.5, 60 ft.**
Follow the crack by the right end.

**133  5.5, 60 ft.**
Climb the corner.

Next comes 400 feet of terraced 5.4–5.6 cliffs (not pictured). It is possible to traverse from climb 128 to the end. Avoid the briers at the bottom. The cliff eventually turns the corner and faces east. Near the end is a 40-foot 5.10 overhang problem (not pictured). From here, continue your bushwhack (you're still less than 25 yards from the trail) and you'll reach:

## Area M

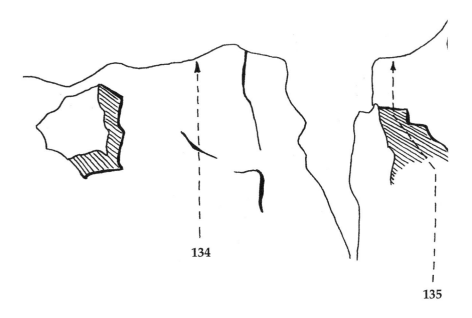

134 **5.7, 40 ft.**
Climb the dirty face to the right of the large block.

135 **5.10, 40 ft.**
Climb the overhang.

136 **5.9, 50 ft.**
Climb the face and the diagonal overhang.

## AREA N

Back on the trail, just past the third falls, are some good bouldering problems (not pictured). The falls themselves have 40- to 70-foot runnels some winters.

## Area M

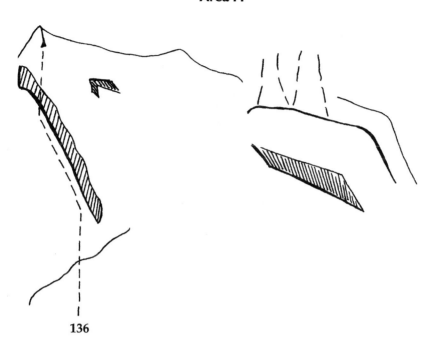

## AREA O

This north-facing cliff is on the left of the path.

137  **5.6, 22 ft.**
     Climb the leaning face.

138  **5.4, 20 ft.**
     Climb the wide chimney.

139  **5.8, 20 ft.**
     Climb the blank wall to the right of the chimney.

140  **5.8, 20 ft.**
     Climb the leaning face.

The cliff continues, but the trail turns away. A large wet section leads to:

## Area O

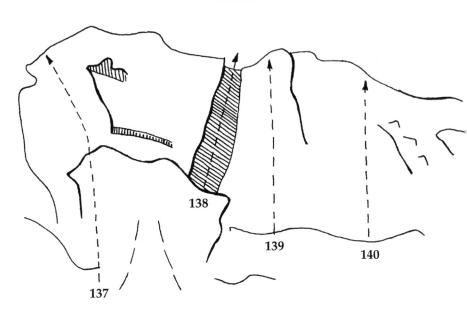

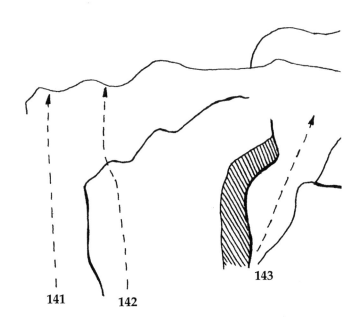

**141  45 ft.**
Too wet for climbing, but occasionally a nice ice route.

**142**  As above.

**143  5.4, 45 ft.**
Climb the face between the overhang and the right flake.

**144  5.9, 45 ft.**
Climb the overhanging face.

**145  5.4, 45 ft.**
Follow the edge up to the left.

**146  5.7, 45 ft.**
Climb the leaning face.

Now comes 60 feet of Grade IV. Go 25 feet past that to good bouldering or go 20 feet back to the trail.

**Area O**

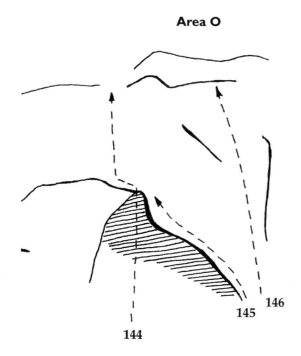

## Area P

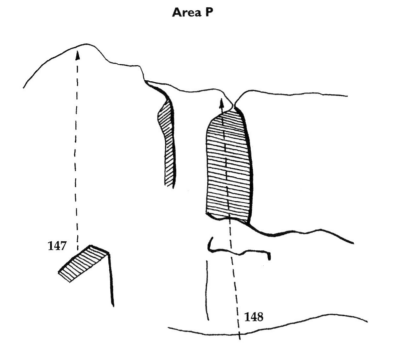

### AREA P

This is a 20-foot north-facing cliff along the trail.

**147  5.6, 20 ft.**
Climb the face.

**148  5.7, 20 ft.**
Climb the edge face.

### AREA Q

From the trail past Area L, look to find:

**149  Garm's Teeth 5.6, 30 ft.**
Follow the wide, deep cracks.

**150  5.6, 30 ft.**
Stay to the right and pass the small overhang.

## Area Q

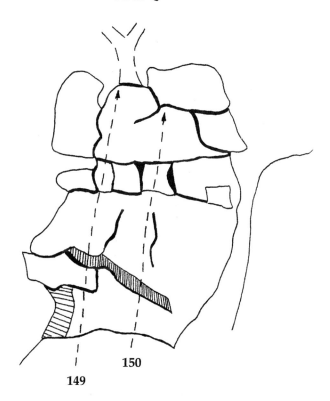

## AREA R

Across the river by the fourth falls are good 40- to 70-foot cliffs (not pictured). Is it worth the bushwhack?

## AREA S

Along the trail, there is good bouldering with west faces.

**151  5.6, 20 ft.**
    Climb the face to the left of the balanced block.

**152  5.5, 20 ft.**
    Climb the corner to the balanced block.

## Area S

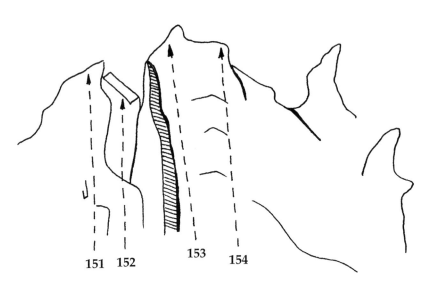

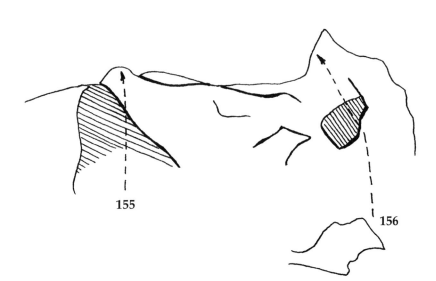

**153  5.9, 20 ft.**
   Follow the vertical outcrop.

**154  5.5, 20 ft.**
   Climb the face to the right of the large outcrop.

The cliff follows the path but loses it at every switchback. There are several good roof problems in this area. Their tops meet the trail. Further down:

**155  5.6, 20 ft.**
   Climb the overhanging edge.

**156  5.7, 30 ft.**
   Do the overhang.

## AREA T

From the trail, by the fourth falls, 60-foot cliffs are visible (not pictured). This is a common camping area, but remember to get a permit. There may be some good routes.

## AREA U

The sixth falls are 50 feet high, and usually have good ice routes, with good cracks for protection (not pictured).

### NEARBY AREAS
See the other chapters on Shenandoah National Park for other options. There is more rock in this area than I've listed here. Bushwhacking in any direction will give you more options. The trails around this area can be easily linked into circuits with Cedar Run Falls or Old Rag Mountain.

### OTHER INFORMATION
Pay the normal Skyline Drive entrance fee. There is another way into this area with no fee, but you'll need a map and will have a long hike. You must have a permit to camp. Bushwhack in the late fall if possible to avoid poison ivy. Be careful around the falls.

• CHAPTER 10 •

# Old Rag Mountain, Rose River Falls

To the climber, Old Rag offers some rare mid-Atlantic granite and some difficult routes up to 150 feet in height. Climbing on Old Rag might not be for everyone. Minuses are a long approach and overcrowding by hikers. According to Shenandoah National Park estimates, over 100,000 people hike up Old Rag every year.

Rose River Falls is a possible but usually poor ice climbing area that also has some climbable rock nearby.

### DIRECTIONS

**Old Rag Mountain.** For the quickest approach, take Route 29 to Sperryville via Route 211-522 and follow 522. Go south on Route 231, turning right onto 643. Continue down 643 (past signs for Old Rag parking). Turn right onto Route 600 and drive to the end of the road (Berry Hollow Fire Road). Hike up the fire road 1.8 miles to the trail. From here it's 0.4 mile to Old Rag Shelter (and spring) and 2 miles to the summit. The trails are clearly marked with blue blazes. There are four distinct groups of cliffs: (1) Behind Byrd's Nest Shelter; (2) on the northwest side, just below the summit; (3) on the northeast side of the summit; and (4) on the southeast side, in a straight line across from the Byrd's Nest Shelter. Old Rag is untapped, with a large number of possible routes and many bouldering problems.

**Rose River Falls, Climbing Rose Falls, Buzzard Rocks.** Reach Rose River Falls by taking Route 29 to Sperryville via Route 211-522 and follow 522. Go south on Route 231, turning right onto 643. Continue down 643 until you hit 600. Turn left (away from Old Rag) and continue until you reach the town of Syria. At Syria, turn right onto 670. Follow 670 to the end, where there is a gate blocking the Rose River Fire Road. Follow the trails to Rose River Falls or bushwhack to Climbing Rose Falls or Buzzard Rocks.

## ROUTE DESCRIPTIONS

## OLD RAG MOUNTAIN

### Area A
The cliffs behind Byrd's Nest Shelter are 40 yards to the left as you face the opening of the shelter.

1. **5.9, 35 ft.**
   Climb the smooth face to the overhanging block.

2. **5.8, 20 ft.**
   Climb the center of the cliff to the left of the scar.

3. **5.6, 20 ft.**
   Follow the scar that widens to a finger crack.

**OLD RAG MOUNTAIN CLIMBING AREAS**

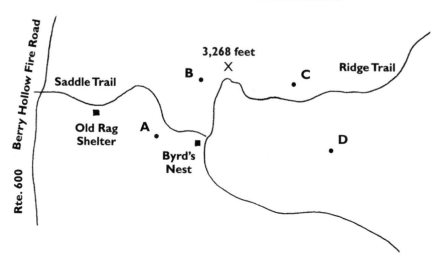

## OLD RAG

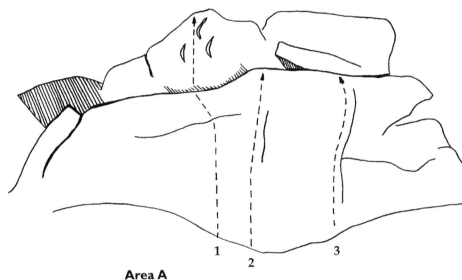

**Area A**

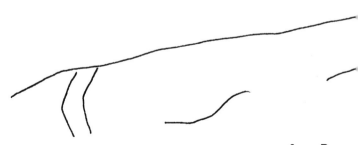

**Area B**

## Area B

These cliffs are on the northwest side of the summit. Bushwhack off the trail near the summit. Check the view from the summit, and you will see the easiest path.

4   **Sunshine Buttress 5.5–5.9, 30–70 ft.**
    Dozens of routes are located on the south-facing side of this buttress. The two cracks are recommended, as well as a traverse along the horizontal crack.

5   **Vice Squad 5.11, 50 ft.**
    Follow the thin diagonal crack.

6   **25–75 ft.**
    Interesting cliff containing a variety of cracks.

7   **5.11, 20 ft. with an 8-ft overhang.**
    A fantastic bouldering problem, close to the trail.

**OLD RAG**

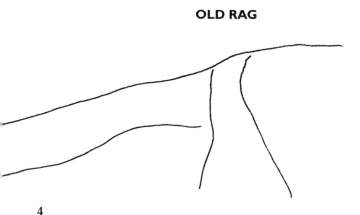

4

## OLD RAG

6   Area B

# OLD RAG

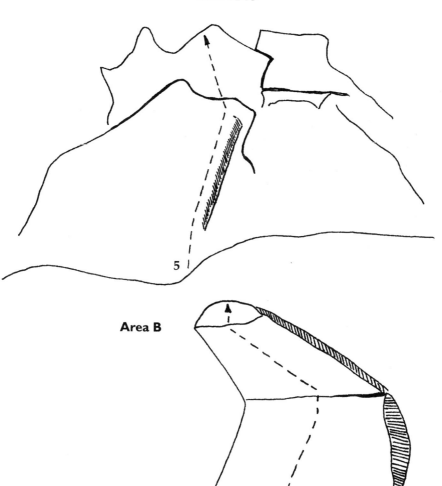

## OLD RAG

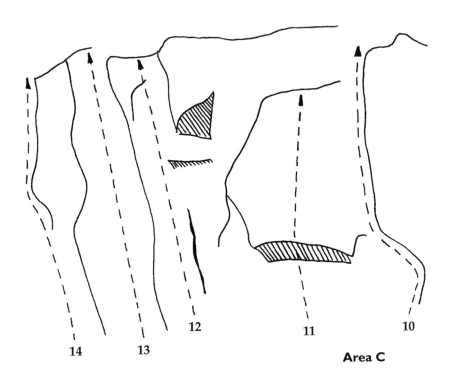

### Area C
At Skyline Wall, the cliffs are on the northeast side of the summit. Follow the ridge trail away from the summit. When the ridge trail passes over large boulders, find a good walkdown area. Head left or right along Skyline Wall.

8 **5.10, 40 ft.**
Climb the overhanging slab.

9 **5.6, 35 ft.**
Climb the leaning slab, following the thin crack.

10 **5.6, 40 ft.**
Climb the crack to the right of the slight overhang.

## OLD RAG

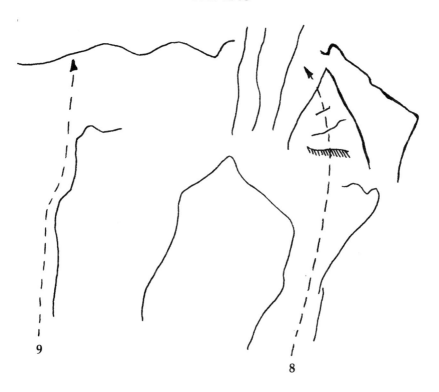

11  **5.8, 40 ft.**
Climb the center of the low overhang.

12  **5.7, 40 ft.**
Follow the cracks to the right of the corner.

13  **5.9, 40 ft.**
Climb the smooth wall to the right of the corner.

14  **5.9, 40 ft.**
Climb the corner.

15  **5.10+, 60 ft.**
Climb the smooth overhanging edge.

# OLD RAG

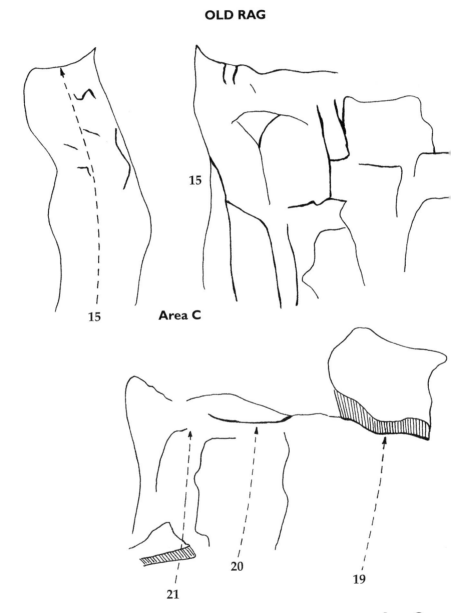

Area C

Area C

Old Rag Mountain, Rose River Falls • 149

16   **5.9, 65 ft.**
Follow the route defined by the Lost Arrows.

17   **5.9, 70 ft.**
Follow the cracks.

18   **5.9, 70 ft.**
Climb up the slab, past the overhang.

19   **Introspection 5.11, 90 ft.**
Follow the bolt line up the smooth slab.

20   **5.7, 75 ft.**
Climb the hand or finger crack.

21   **Project 5.10?, 75 ft.***
Climb the smooth wall to the left of the thin crack. (Was this project finished in the summer of '96?)

**OLD RAG**

*A project is an uncompleted route that has no rating or name until it is climbed.

## Area D

These are cliffs on the southeast side of the summit. Veer off the ridge trail and head down to the cliffs. It is also possible to bushwhack straight over from the Bryd's Nest Shelter to this area. Bring the topo map to be safe.

22  **Oh My God Corner 5.10b, 70 ft.**
    Climb the dihedral.

23  **Eagle's Gift 5.9, 120 ft.**
    Climb the difficult face.

24  **Bushwhack Crack 5.10c, 75 ft.**
    Follow the hand crack through the overhang.

Not shown:

25  **Strawberry Fields 5.11a, 130 ft.**
    Located uphill to the right of climb 22. Climb the easy hand crack that thins to a treacherous face.

**OLD RAG**

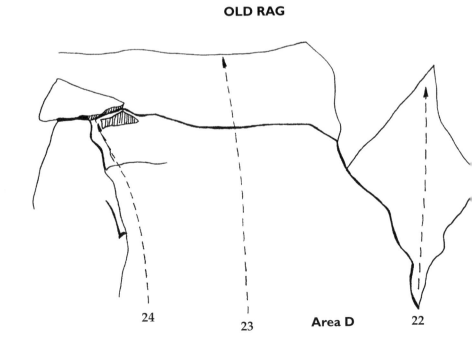

26  **Good Friday 5.11, 80 ft.**
Multiwidth crack located down past climb 24.

27  **April Fool 5.11, 55 ft.**
Thin diagonal crack to the left of climb 26.

## NEARBY AREAS

Both the Cedar Run Falls and White Oak Canyon Trails can be made into circuit hikes linking up with Old Rag Mountain. See the chapters dealing with these areas as well as the other chapters on Shenandoah National Park.

Dark Hollow Falls is also rumored to have some good climbing and a waterfall with a 70-foot drop. Reach it by parking at Skyline Drive mile marker 50.7 and following the marked trail 0.8 mile. This trail can also be done as a circuit hike combining the Rose River Falls trails.

## OTHER INFORMATION

All Shenandoah National Park regulations are in effect, as well as some special Old Rag regulations. No dogs or bikes are allowed on the mountain. No camping is allowed above the Byrd's Nest Shelter. Free permits are necessary for overnight camping and can be obtained from any park ranger station or by writing. Stay away from Old Rag between Memorial Day and Labor Day to avoid the crowds, but if challenging granite sounds inviting, Old Rag is for you. The climbing areas are away from the crowds, and you will find only the occasional climber. For the uninitiated, granite is extremely rough. Remember tape for the hands and a good abrasion kit. Expect high winds and sudden cold weather in the early spring and late fall.

# CHAPTER 13

# Cedar Run Falls, Half-Mile Cliff

Cedar Run Falls has climbing similar to that at nearby White Oak Canyon. Expect smaller routes (up to 45 feet in height) than White Oak Canyon, but look for the same type of problems.

Half-Mile Cliff lives up to its name. It is a 70- to 90-foot cliff face over half a mile long, located toward the bottom of Cedar Run Canyon. It should actually be called Hard-Access Cliff. Some routes have been done around the terraced face, but you have many better options elsewhere in the park.

## DIRECTIONS

Several paths and trails lead to Cedar Run Falls, but to use the shortest, park at the Hawksbill Gap parking lot at Skyline Drive mile marker 45.6 on the east side of the road. Follow the marked trail down to the falls. The rocks are listed in the order that you will come to them. The trail links up with some other good areas, but unless you plan to camp, retrace your steps to the parking area. Half-Mile Cliff is toward the bottom of the canyon. To reach Half-Mile Cliff, find the spot where the trail crosses the river for the second time and veers away from the path. Stay on the east side and head down the river. Half-Mile Cliff is on the ridge above the river.

## ROUTE DESCRIPTIONS

### CEDAR RUN FALLS

#### Area A

As you head down the east side of the path, look for the first group of boulders. At this point, bushwhack east 50 yards to a west-facing crag.

1. **5.10, 30 ft.**
   Climb the smooth edge.

2. **5.9, 35 ft.**
   Climb up the center of the face.

On the south-facing side:

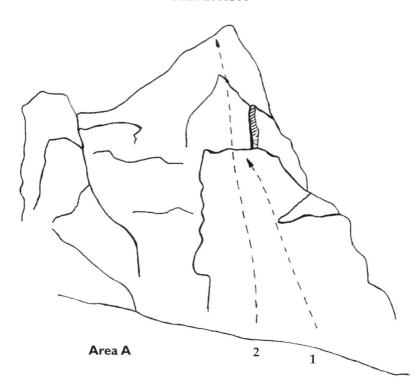

**CEDAR RUN**

Area A

## CEDAR RUN

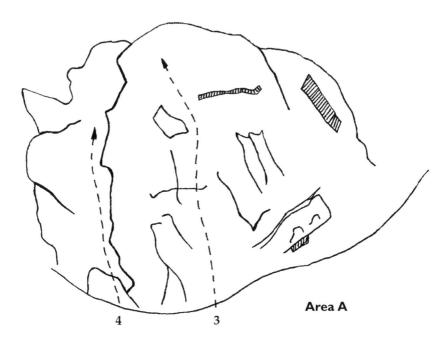

Area A

3  **5.6, 45 ft.**
   Climb the cracked face.

4  **5.4, 45 ft.**
   Follow the edge.

### Area B
This is another west-facing cliff along the trail, just down from Area A.

5  **5.11, 25 ft.**
   Difficult roof problem.

6  **5.4, 20 ft.**
   Avoid the roofs by passing between them.

7  **5.9, 28 ft.**
   Climb the leaning slabs.

# CEDAR RUN

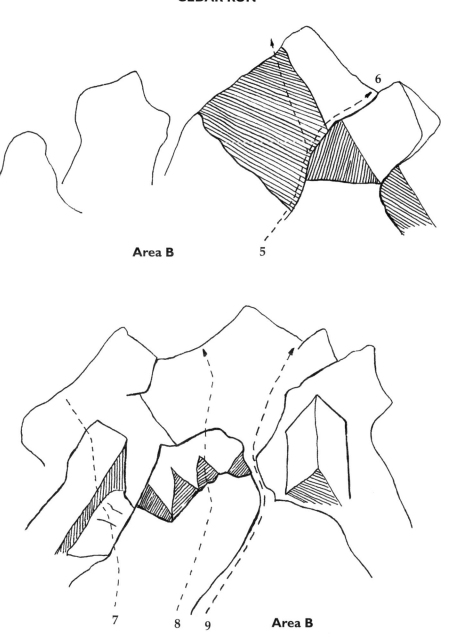

8   **Jagged Teeth 5.10, 30 ft.**
    Climb the leaning faces and go over the pointy overhang.

9   **5.8, 30 ft.**
    Climb the face between the teeth overhang and the outcropping.

10  **10-ft. ceiling project**

This same area turns away from the path and becomes a south-facing crag.

11  **5.8, 25 ft.**
    Climb anywhere on this face.

Further down, the crag turns and becomes a north-facing cliff.

12  **5.11, 20 ft.**
    Difficult leaning face (a boulder obstructs the view).

13  **5.12, 20 ft.**
    Roof problem.

**CEDAR RUN**

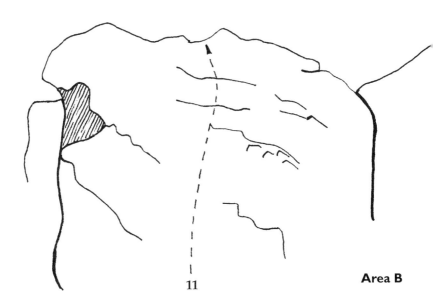

Area B

## CEDAR RUN

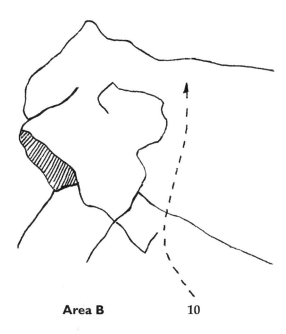

**Area B**   10

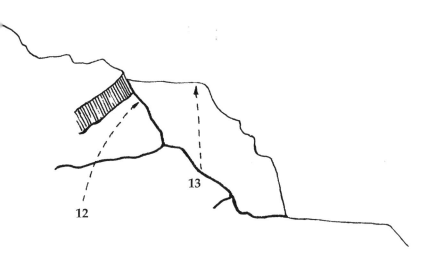

12   13

## CEDAR RUN

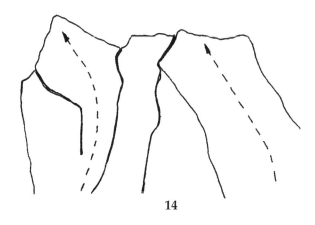

**Area B**

Behind climbs 12 and 13 is a 20-foot wall (south facing) with 5.5 crack routes (not pictured). Bushwhacking 50 feet from this point brings you to a good bouldering area (not pictured).

Further down the path:

**14  5.10, 18 ft.**
   Two leaning west-facing routes.

### Area C

Along the path, look for large boulders close to the stream. Try this spot in late July or early August. Most other times of the year, it is damp. On the west-facing side:

**15  5.11-, 20 ft.**
   Climb the leaning face.

## CEDAR RUN

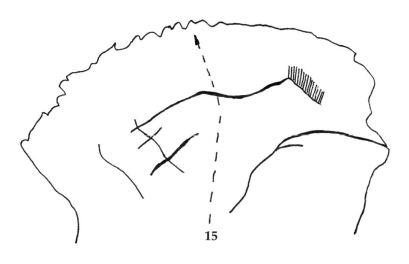

**Area C**

On the south-facing side:

16  **5.10, 25 ft.**
    To the left of the cave entrance, climb the face.

17  **Project 5.13?, 16 ft.**
    Climb the ceiling up out of the cave.

18  **5.9, 20 ft.**
    Climb the east-facing wall in the cave and continue up through the chimney.

Also, there is a good 18-foot bouldering wall on the southwest-facing side of the cave entrance.

## CEDAR RUN

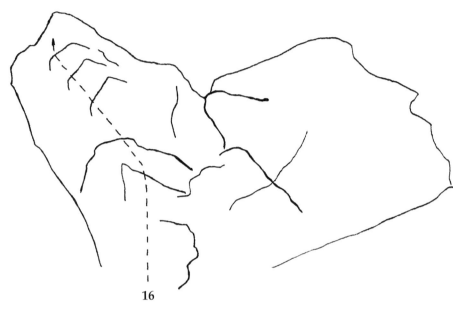

16

### Area C

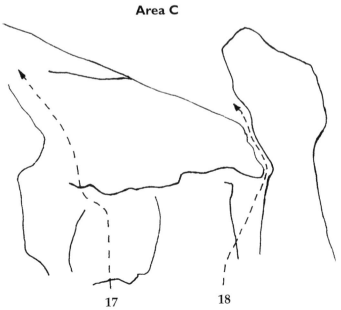

17    18

## NEARBY AREAS

There are nearby climbing areas all along Skyline Drive, but especially Old Rag and White Oak Canyon, whose trails link up with Cedar Run Falls. See the other chapters on Shenandoah National Park for more climbing options.

## OTHER INFORMATION

All Shenandoah National Park and Skyline Drive rules and regulations are in effect. See Appendix B for more information. Check with the rangers, because camping in this area is often closed.

• CHAPTER 12 •

# Hawksbill Summit, Franklin Cliffs

At 4,050 feet, Hawksbill Summit is one of the tallest points on Skyline Drive. A short hike to the peak brings you to greenstone cliffs up to 70 feet in height. This mountain has great views of Old Rag, Crescent Rocks, and, on clear days, Washington, D.C. Hawksbill Summit was also the site of the peregrine falcon reintroduction to the park in the early nineties.

Trash-covered Franklin Cliffs are close to Skyline Drive but have little value to climbers. They are extremely friable and overgrown.

### DIRECTIONS

Reach Hawksbill Summit by parking at Hawksbill Gap Parking Area at Skyline Drive mile marker 45.6 on the west side of the drive. (Access to the Cedar Run Falls Trail is across the drive.) Head up the marked trail about 1 mile to the summit.

Reach Franklin Cliffs by parking at its overlook around Skyline Drive mile marker 48.7. The cliffs are below the parking area.

## HAWKSBILL CLIMBING AREAS

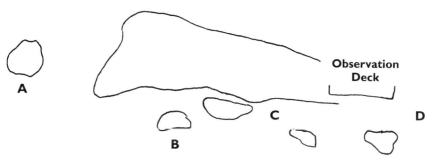

## ROUTE DESCRIPTIONS

### HAWKSBILL SUMMIT

### Area A

Reach this area by going (the easy way) around the observation deck and finding a walkdown. This puts you at the easternmost point of the summit. The climbs are listed going east to west. On the northeast-facing side:

1. **5.7, 22 ft.**
   Climb the leaning slab.

2. **5.9, 22 ft.**
   Climb the underhanging slab.

3. **5.4, 22 ft.**
   To the right of the boulder separation, climb the easy face.

4. **5.7, 22 ft.**
   To the right of the boulder separation, climb the face.

On the north-facing side:

5. **5.4, 30 ft.**
   Climb the easy face.

# HAWKSBILL

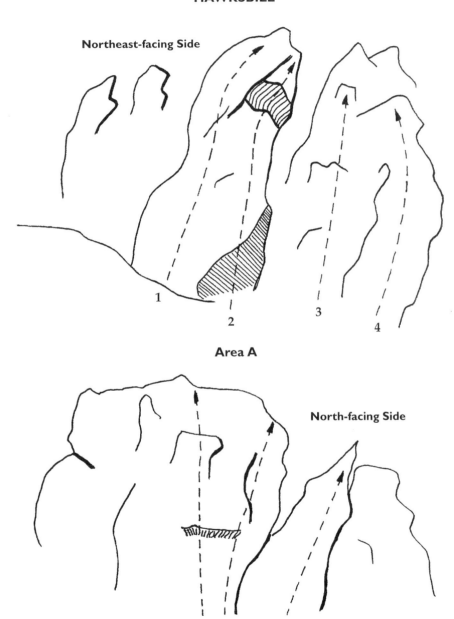

Area A

6  **5.6, 30 ft.**
   Close to the edge of the 30-foot boulder, climb the face.

7  **5.3, 18 ft.**
   Climb the easy route on the lower boulder.

### Area B
There is a 30-foot boulder in front of the main cliff.

8  **5.9, 30 ft.**
   On the northwest-facing side, climb the leaning route up the center of the boulder.

9  **5.7, 30 ft.**
   On the north-facing side, follow the crack.

**HAWKSBILL**

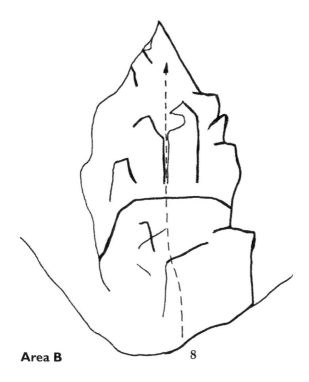

**Area B**      8

## HAWKSBILL

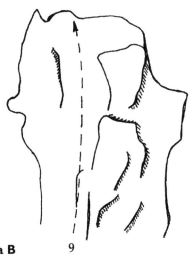

**Area B**  9

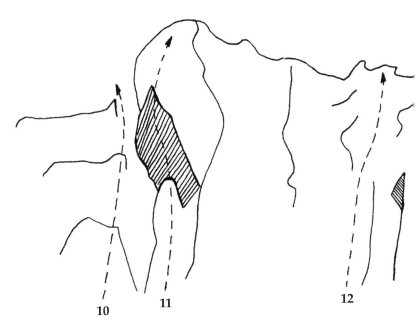

10  11  12

**Area C: Main Section**

## Area C

This is the main section.

10. **5.7, 70 ft.**
    Climb the face to the left of the chimney.

11. **5.10, 70 ft.**
    To the right of the chimney, climb the overhanging face.

12. **5.7, 45 ft.**
    Climb the face.

13. **5.8, 45 ft.**
    In the center of the small outcropped block, climb the face.

14. **5.7, 45 ft.**
    Climb the face.

**HAWKSBILL**

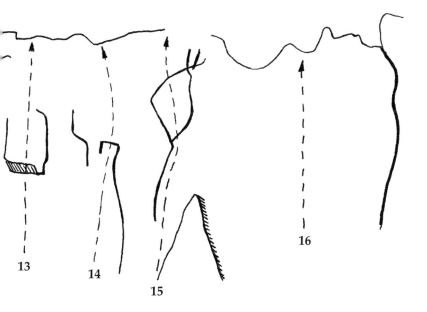

# HAWKSBILL

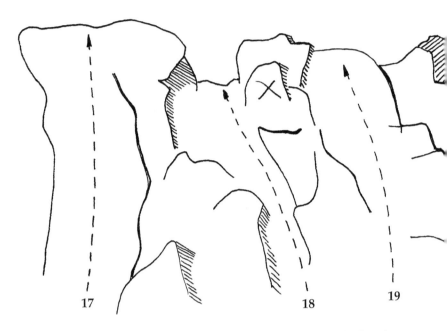

**Area C: Main Section**

15  **5.7, 45 ft.**
    Follow the cracks.

16  **5.2–5.4, 45 ft.**
    To the right of the cracks, climb this easy face anywhere.

17  **5.4, 50 ft.**
    Follow the hand crack.

18  **5.7, 40 ft.**
    Approximately 25 feet to the right of climb 17, climb the leaning ramp.

19  **5.7, 40 ft.**
    Climb the face.

## HAWKSBILL

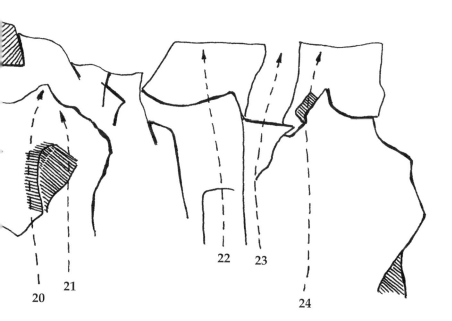

20  **5.10, 35 ft.**
Starting at the low overhang, climb the leaning slab.

21  **5.8, 35 ft.**
Climb the leaning face.

22  **5.6, 35 ft.**
In front of the detached block, climb the face.

23  **5.4, 35 ft.**
Follow the crack and finish through the chimney.

24  **5.7, 35 ft.**
Climb the face around the overhanging rocks.

From here, it is easy to head back up the trail. You are about 20 feet southwest of the Byrd's Nest Shelter.

## Area D
Further down past Area C:

**25  5.7, 40 ft.**
Climb anywhere on the center of this north-facing cliff.

When leaving the summit, hike down the Appalachian Trail 0.9 mile to the parking lot. This alternative route leads you past more areas and gives you good views of the rocks at the summit. You could go up the trail to reach these rocks, but the summit trail is quicker

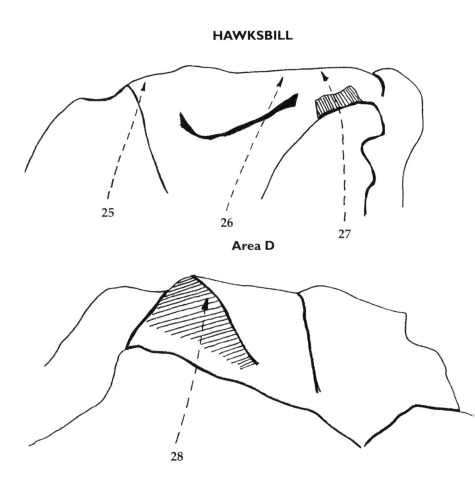

**HAWKSBILL**

**Area D**

(and safer) than scrambling up scree slopes. Many of the areas along this route are damp. Pictured are two good bouldering areas on the right side of the path. As usual, the climbs are listed as you will come to them.

**26   5.8, 25 ft.**
   To the right of the large undercling, climb the face.

**27   5.8, 25 ft.**
   On the left, downhill side, climb the face.

**28   5.4–5.7, 40 ft.**
   Climb anywhere on this face.

## NEARBY AREAS

See the other chapters on Shenandoah National Park for more climbing options.

## OTHER INFORMATION

See Appendix B for rules, regulations, and camping options.

• CHAPTER 13 •

# Blackrock, Split Rock, Lewis Falls

Blackrock has a decent variety of top-roping routes and bouldering problems up to 50 feet in height. Its close proximity to Big Meadows Lodge provides quick access to climbing and large amounts of trash dropped over the cliff face by tourists. In addition, this is one of the few climbing areas where you can be straining for your next fingerhold and hear "Johnson party of six, your table is ready."

Split Rock is a nice little crag less than 100 yards from Skyline Drive. It's a great place for a lazy afternoon of bouldering and picnicking. Split Rock reaches heights of 40 feet and has a few good routes, some wide cracks, and odd-shaped chimneys.

Lewis Falls cascades down about 70 feet. Is there ever good ice at Lewis Falls? Some old-timers say yes, but the conditions (wet fall, cold winter) must be perfect. Lewis Falls and the surrounding rocks are not pictured.

### DIRECTIONS

**Blackrock.** Pull off Skyline Drive at mile marker 51 and park in the back by Big Meadows Lodge. The cliffs and the Appalachian Trail are directly below the lodge, and several paths lead down to them. At certain times of the year, Big Meadows Lodge and the roads around it might be closed. Simply park at Fishers Gap Overlook (Skyline Drive mile marker 49.3) and head south on the Appalachian Trail.

**Split Rock.** Park in the Fishers Gap Overlook at Skyline Drive mile marker 49.3. Follow signs to the Appalachian Trail and travel south (the Appalachian Trail is marked by white blazes, so do not follow the blue blazes). You'll reach Split Rock on your left, in under 0.2 mile. Continuing down the Appalachian Trail from this point takes you to both Monkey's Head and Blackrock in under 1.25 miles.

**Lewis Falls.** From the Amphitheater in Big Meadows Campground, follow the Appalachian Trail south for 0.1 mile to a trail intersection. At this intersection, follow the marked downhill trail just over a mile to the falls. Monkey's Head is a small rock outcropping behind Big Meadows Campground. It has a couple of intermediate 25-foot boulder problems on its west and north sides. Monkey's Head is not pictured but is included due to its closeness to the major Shenandoah National Park campground.

## ROUTE DESCRIPTIONS

### BLACKROCK LOWER CLIFF

This set of rocks is below the main crags and the Appalachian Trail. These are short north- and northwest-facing routes.

1  **5.8, 20 ft.**
   Climb the face to the left of the crack.

2  **5.5, 20 ft.**
   Head up the wide crack.

3  **5.6, 20 ft.**
   Climb the face to the right of the crack.

4  **5.5, 20 ft.**
   To the right of the low outcrop, climb the flat face.

5  **5.7, 20 ft.**
   Climb the outcropping ledges.

## BLACKROCK

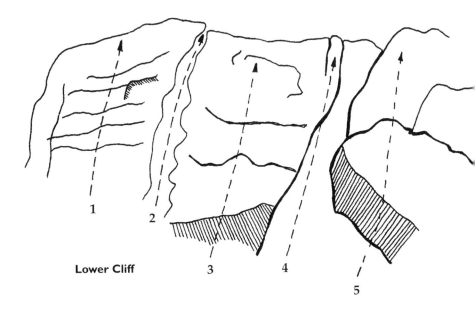

**Lower Cliff**

### BLACKROCK MAIN SECTION

From south to north:

6  **5.6, 50 ft.**
   Climb the scarred face to the right of the ramp.

7  **5.7, 30 ft.**
   To the left of the ramp, climb the face.

8  **5.10, 30 ft.**
   Climb the overhang.

9  **5.9, 30 ft.**
   Climb the small overhang to the left of the large outcrop.

10 **5.10, 30 ft.**
   Climb the leaning face.

## BLACKROCK

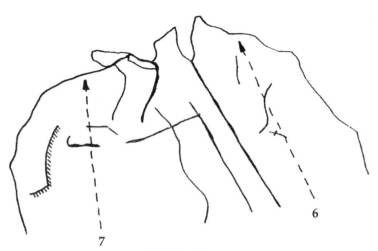

**Main Section**

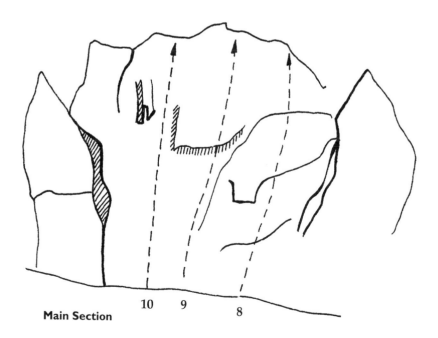

**Main Section**

# BLACKROCK

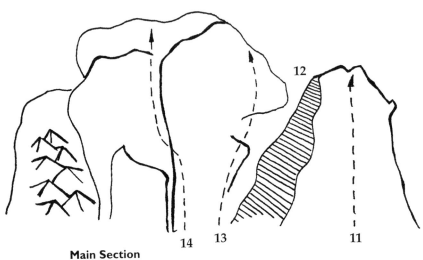

Main Section

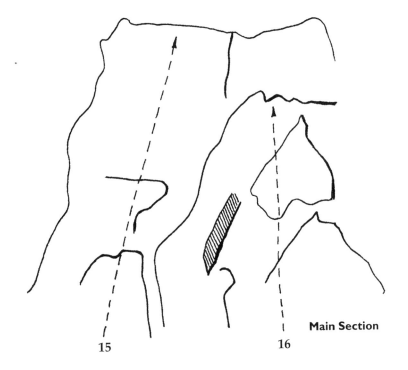

Main Section

Blackrock, Split Rock, Lewis Falls • 177

11  **5.5, 40 ft.**
    Climb the flat dihedral.

12  **5.2, 40 ft.**
    Climb the chimney.

13  **5.10, 45 ft.**
    Climb the leaning face to the left of the chimney.

14  **5.7, 45 ft.**
    Follow the ledge and crack.

15  **5.4, 40 ft.**
    Make your way around the ledges and overhangs.

16  **5.4, 40 ft.**
    Climb anywhere on the easy face.

The detached block has bouldering problems on two or three sides. Only the tallest side is shown.

**BLACKROCK**

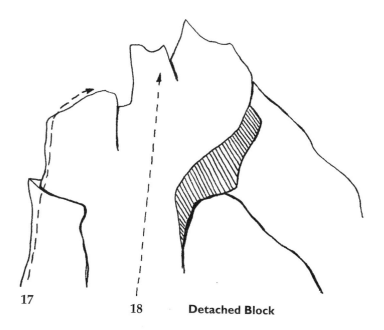

17    18    **Detached Block**

17   **5.6, 20 ft.**
     Go up the center.

18   **5.8, 20 ft.**
     Climb the corner.

Continuing on the Blackrock main cliff:

19   **5.7, 40 ft.**
     Climb past the cracks and up the face.

20   **5.2, 30 ft.**
     Climb the easy face.

21   **5.5, 30 ft.**
     Climb past the diagonal crack.

22   **5.7, 30 ft.**
     Start at the lower overhangs and follow the cracks.

**BLACKROCK**

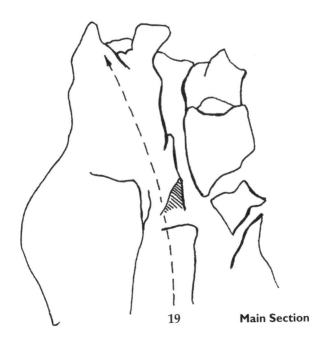

19         **Main Section**

## BLACKROCK

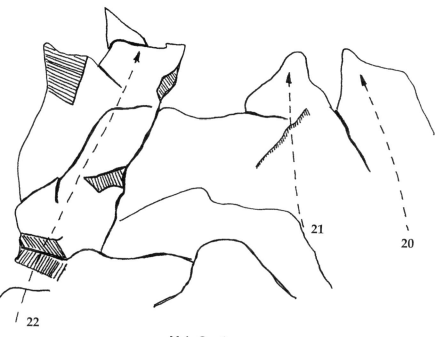

**Main Section**

## FISHERS WALL

The faces of these northwest rocks are visible from the trail. Descriptions for Fishers Wall go from north to south.

1. **Split Chimney 5.5, 36 ft.**
   Climb the angled chimney.

2. **5.7, 40 ft.**
   To the right of Split Chimney, climb the easy face.

3. **Fishers Face 5.9, 40 ft.**
   Climb the blank face in the center of the left section.

## SPLIT ROCK

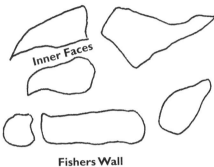

## FISHERS WALL

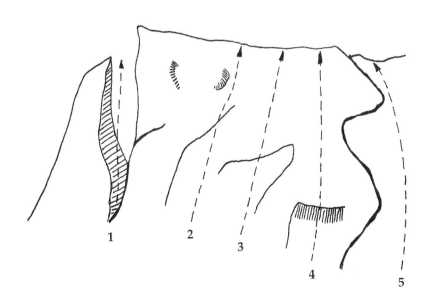

4   **Fisher's Whiskers 5.11, 40 ft.**
    Climb the smooth face starting at the low overhang.

5   **5.8, 40 ft.**
    Climb the corner separating the left section of Fishers Wall with the lower sections.

On the center section:

6   **Diamond of Aces 5.9, 30 ft.**
    Climb the leaning center section.

On the right section:

7   **Bouldering?**

On the inner faces, three good routes have been done:

**FISHERS WALL**

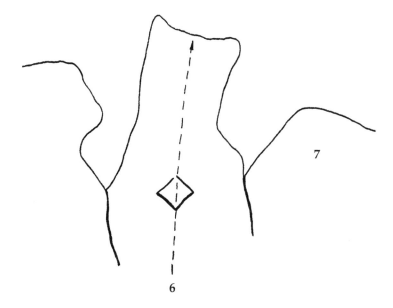

## FISHERS WALL

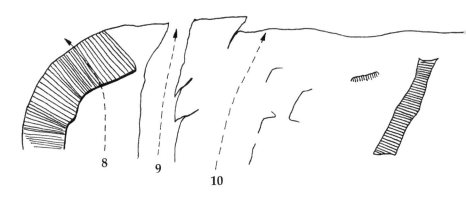

**Inner Faces**

8  **5.10, 18 ft.**
   Climb the short, steep overhang.

9  **5.4, 40 ft.**
   Climb the leaning chimney.

10 **5.6, 30 ft.**
   On the right of the chimney, climb the leaning face.

### NEARBY AREAS

See the other chapters on Shenandoah National Park for nearby climbing options.

### OTHER INFORMATION

Typical rules and regulations for Shenandoah National Park apply (see Appendix B).

# • CHAPTER 14 •

# Bearfence Mountain, South River Falls

Bearfence Mountain is the best bouldering area in Virginia. It has a short access, climbs up to 40 feet in height, and a variety of difficult routes guaranteed to whip you into shape. If you don't hang out in climbing gyms, bouldering should be high on your list. It's the best way to develop the skills and strengths necessary to move up the grades. The summit of Bearfence Mountain offers a 360-degree view of the Shenandoah Valley.

South River Falls is one of the most scenic and tallest (83 feet) falls in the park. They are located in a beautiful canyon 1.3 miles from the parking area. Ice runnels form occasionally. The cliffs across from the falls are climbable. However, like many cliffs by waterfalls, they are damp and mossy in sections.

## DIRECTIONS

The Bearfence Parking Area is at Skyline Drive mile marker 56.4. Follow the marked trail 200 yards up toward the Appalachian Trail. For the closest approach to the rocks, follow the Appalachian Trail instead of the Bearfence Loop. The rocks are on your left, and the entire loop is less than 700 yards.

Reach the South River Falls area by parking at the South River Falls Picnic Area located at Skyline Drive mile marker 62.8. Follow the marked trail 1.3 miles down the canyon to the waterfall. The trail continues, but it will be quicker to backtrack when you leave.

## ROUTE DESCRIPTIONS

### BEARFENCE MOUNTAIN: BEAR PAW ROCK

1. **Bear Paw 5.8, 40 ft.**
   Climb the edge.

2. **Pooh Bear 5.10, 40 ft.**
   Climb the center of the separating block.

3. **5.9, 40 ft.**
   Climb the shallow crack at the highest point of the formation.

4. **5.7, 40 ft.**
   Follow the crack separating the fingerlike pinnacles.

5. **Pinkie 5.7, 40 ft.**
   Climb the face on the last finger.

### BEARFENCE MOUNTAIN

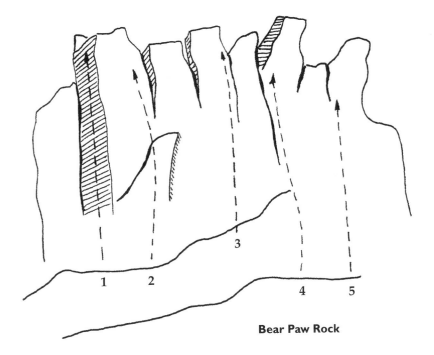

**Bear Paw Rock**

## BEARFENCE MOUNTAIN

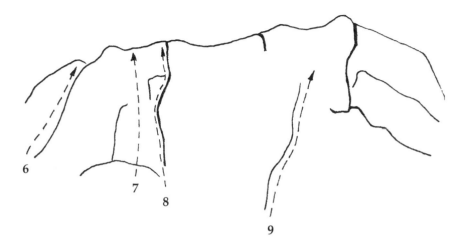

To the right of this formation is an easy path to the upper part of the loop. Continuing down:

6   **5.2, 22 ft.**
Climb the short chimney.

7   **5.6, 22 ft.**
Directly to the right of the long crack, climb the face.

8   **5.2, 22 ft.**
Climb the long crack.

9   **5.5, 22 ft.**
Climb the diagonal crack.

The cliffs taper off for about 100 yards, and when they regain their height, they vary from 35 to 45 feet. They are lichen-covered with large terraces. When the lichen ends:

10  **5.8, 35 ft.**
Follow the crack.

11  **5.10, 35 ft.**
Climb the leaning slab face through the center of the slight overhang.

12  **5.10, 35 ft.**
Climb the face, following the finger crack on the upper section.

13  **5.6, 30 ft.**
Follow the separating edge using layback techniques.

14  **5.10, 30 ft.**
Climb the leaning slab. Stay to the left of the large overhang. Variation: 5.13, 32 ft. Climb the overhang.

15  **5.11, 30 ft.**
Climb the leaning face.

**BEARFENCE MOUNTAIN**

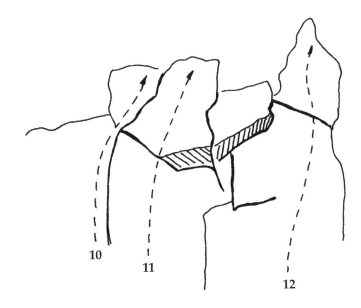

## BEARFENCE MOUNTAIN

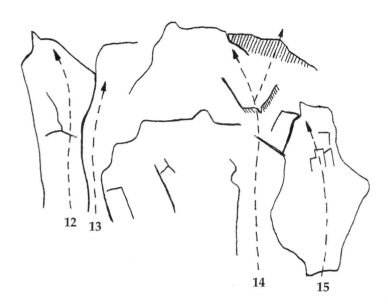

Finally, down by the point where the loop turns to go to both the Appalachian Trail and the upper section of the loop:

16  **5.8, 20 ft.**
    Climb the face.

17  **5.10, 20 ft.**
    Climb the leaning corner.

18  **5.7, 20 ft.**
    To the right of the leaning corner, climb the face.

There are many more bouldering problems in this area, so do some exploring.

## BEARFENCE MOUNTAIN

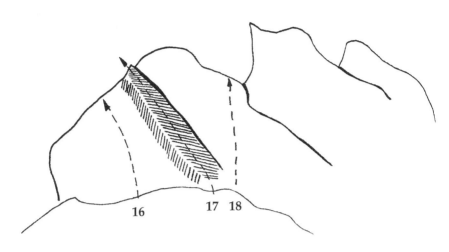

16   17 18

## SOUTH RIVER FALLS

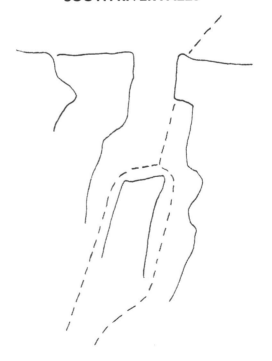

## SOUTH RIVER FALLS

Ice forms on both sides of the falls, but the right side is usually stronger. A pool forms in the center where the falls split.

### NEARBY AREAS

They are many more climbing options along Skyline Drive. See the other chapters dealing with these areas. Other places not listed anywhere else are:

**Rockytop.** From Skyline Drive mile marker 76.2, hike 3.5 miles north on the marked trail to the summit. This is a long ridge of sandstone visible from Skyline Drive.

**Ivy Creek.** Go south from the overlook at Skyline Drive mile marker 77.5 for 1.4 miles. The cliffs are located 0.3 mile from the creek.

### OTHER INFORMATION

See Appendix B for both camping information and the rules and regulations for Shenandoah National Park and the Appalachian Trail.

• CHAPTER 15 •

# Loft Mountain, Calvary Rocks, Chimney Rocks

Loft Mountain has a few great routes 25 to 30 feet in height located along one of the nicest interpretive trails in Shenandoah National Park. There is more rock toward the summit, but none as nice as the pictured routes.

Calvary Rocks and Chimney Rocks have decent bouldering and top-rope routes, but they are nothing special. Expect sandstone blocks with some quartzite reaching heights of 30 feet. Calvary Rocks is a maze of tall blocks, and Chimney Rocks is a cliff face forming a ridge. Chimney Rocks is marked by iron spikes that once formed a bridge support, but it's hard to imagine how massive it must have been. Did it actually cross the valley?

**DIRECTIONS**

Loft Mountain can be reached by parking at Loft Mountain Wayside at Skyline Drive mile marker 79.5. Cross the drive and follow the Deadening Trail to the top of Loft Mountain. The trail is a 1.4-mile circuit and gets its name from a process used to reforest the mountain. The dead American chestnuts along the trail were not killed by the blight but rather by deadening in the 1930s. The idea was to chop the trees enough to kill them, but not enough to make them fall. The reduction of foliage would allow smaller trees, grasses, and bushes to take root, which would increase the wildlife in the area. Set fires are the modern equivalent of the deadening process. Newer trees never grew in this area, because the chestnut blight wiped out all the immature trees.

Calvary Rocks and Chimney Rocks can be reached by parking at Skyline Drive mile marker 90. Hike up the trail 0.4 mile from the parking lot to the Riprap Trail. Turn left at the first milepost and follow the trail 1 mile to Calvary Rocks. The Chimney Rocks area is further down the trail. Neither Calvary Rocks nor Chimney Rocks is pictured.

## ROUTE DESCRIPTIONS

### LOFT MOUNTAIN

Along the Deadening Trail:

1  **5.12, 25 ft.**
   Climb the leaning roof overhang.

2  **5.12+, 25 ft.**
   Climb the leaning roof at its widest point.

At the second roof area:

3  **5.13, 25 ft.**
   Climb the leaning roof.

4  **5.7, 25 ft.**
   Pass between the overhangs.

5  **5.9, 25 ft.**
   At the smaller roof section, climb the leaning face.

6  **5.8, 25 ft.**
   At the short end, climb the face.

There are more routes up the trail by the summit, including a short, thin, diagonal crack. The trail is a circuit, and you are past the halfway point, so continue on the trail to return to the wayside.

## LOFT MOUNTAIN

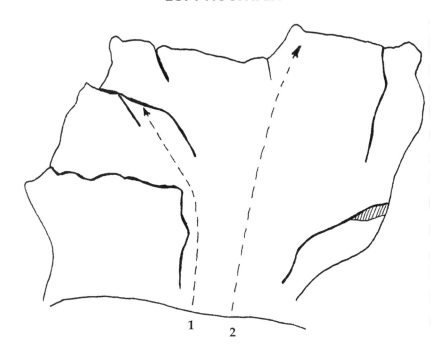

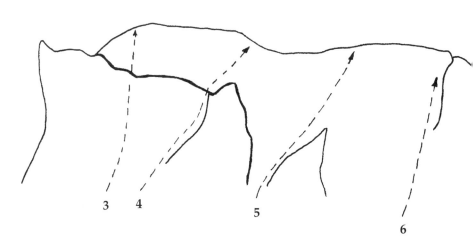

## NEARBY AREAS

There are many more climbing options along Skyline Drive and in Shenandoah National Park. See the other chapters in this part for more information. Some other nearby areas include:

**Doyles River and Jones Run Falls.** Located at Skyline Drive mile marker 81.1. There are possible ice routes, and Doyles River is rumored to have some good bouldering options. Both involve long hikes.

**Blackrock.** Located at Skyline Drive mile marker 84.8. Do not confuse this area with the great area mentioned in Chapter 13. This was once a great cliff, but it has broken down into a talus slope over the last million years or so. The remaining cliffs are about 10 feet tall, but the pile of rubble is impressive.

**Turk Gap and Turk Mountain.** Located 2 miles down the trail from Skyline Drive mile marker 94.1, these areas are rumored to have good bouldering.

## OTHER INFORMATION

See Appendix B for information on camping options and park regulations.

# PART IV

# George Washington National Forest

# • CHAPTER 16 •

# Elizabeth Furnace Areas: Talking Headwall, Buzzard Rocks (Little El Cap)

This is another great but virtually undiscovered climbing area, and it's not too far from northern Virginia. These areas are all located around the Elizabeth Furnace camping area.

The Talking Headwall is a crag close to the road along the entrance to Elizabeth Furnace. It has a series of hard overhangs and leaning face routes. The crag reaches 45 feet in height.

It is called Buzzard Rocks on the map, but climbers have named it Little El Cap. You will find it high on the ridge top of Massanutten Mountain overlooking Passage Creek. Passage Creek is good for canoeing, trout fishing, and after-climb dips. The cliffs can top 110 feet, but most routes are shorter. It takes some dedication to reach the top.

## DIRECTIONS

Reach Elizabeth Furnace by taking Route 55 west from Front Royal. Follow 55 west to the town of Waterlick. Tun left onto Powells Fort Road (Route 678). Talking Headwall is on the right side of the road about 2 miles from Route 55. At the point where the cliff face meets the road, find a pull-off area and park. Walk back up the road and follow the cliff as it turns toward the woods and away from the road.

From this point, you should have a good view of Little El Cap and the ridge across from Talking Headwall. You have three choices to reach this rock: (1) Draw a straight line and hike up the scree slope. (2) Drive back up Route 678 and turn into the fish hatchery. Park at the hatchery and follow the orange-blazed Massanutten Mountain East Trail up the ridge top. (3) The longest but easiest route is to park at the Elizabeth Furnace Picnic Area and follow the Big Blue Trail to Shawl Gap. At Shawl Gap, head north on the Massanutten Mountain East Trail. Whichever route you pick, bring water.

## ROUTE DESCRIPTIONS

### LITTLE EL CAP

From south to north along the ridge top:

1. **5.9, 50 ft.**
   Climb the leaning slab.

2. **5.8, 55 ft.**
   Climb the face to the left of the leaning slab.

3. **5.8, 85 ft.**
   Climb the center of the protruding face.

### LITTLE EL CAP

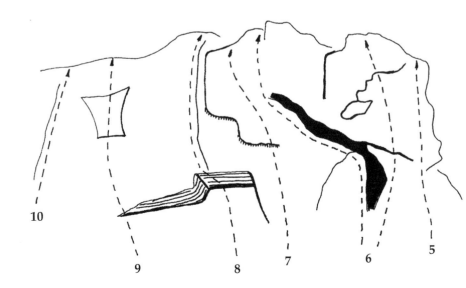

4   **5.9, 85 ft.**
    Climb the thin cracks along the edge of the protruding face.

Further north along the ridge:

5   **5.12, 85 ft.**
    Climb the smooth face.

6   **5.11, 85 ft.**
    Climb the leaning face.

7   **5.10, 90 ft.**
    Follow the crack around the overhanging slab.

8   **5.11, 90 ft.**
    Climb the face to the left of the slab.

9   **5.10, 85 ft.**
    Climb through the center of the depression and up over the overhang.

## LITTLE EL CAP

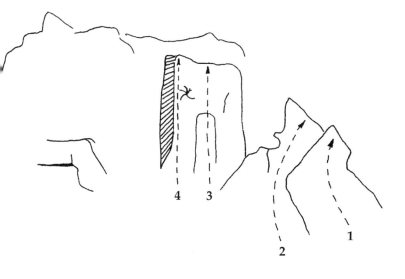

## LITTLE EL CAP

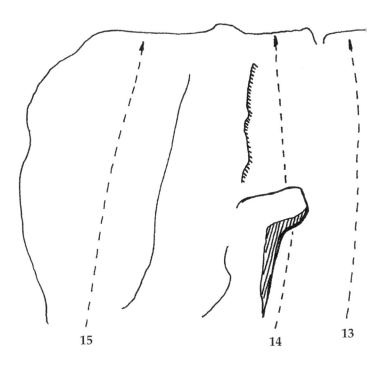

10  **5.9, 75 ft.**
Climb the face up past the left edge of the overhang and over the detached block.

11  **5.9, 75 ft.**
Follow the crack.

12  **5.9, 75 ft.**
Climb the face, passing over the slight overhang.

13  **5.9, 75 ft.**
To the right, climb the flake.

## LITTLE EL CAP

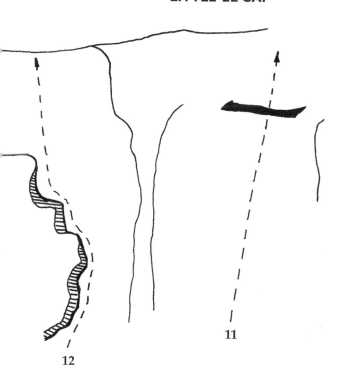

**14** 5.10, 75 ft.
Climb the face formed by the separating face.

**15** 5.10, 75 ft.
Climb the face, passing beneath the large outcropping, and continue up along the edge.

**16** 5.9, 70 ft.
Climb the smooth face.

Still further north along the ridge, two cliffs are obscured by trees except during the winter. They are 40 feet high and have several routes ranging from 5.5 to 5.9. They are not pictured.

## TALKING HEADWALL

The routes are listed along the short trail, starting at the point farthest from the road.

At the northern end, east-facing cliff:

1. **5.11, 20 ft.**
   Climb the terraced slab and the overhang.
2. **5.10, 25 ft.**
   Climb the thin space between the overhangs.

**TALKING HEADWALL**

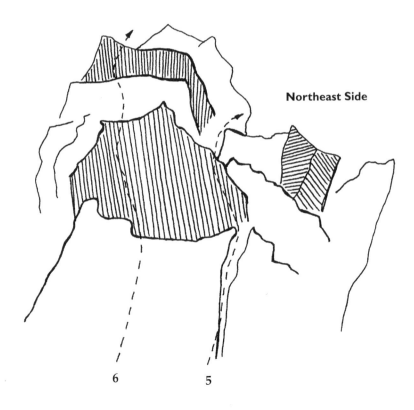

3   **5.11, 25 ft.**
    Follow the thin crack and finish by climbing the tall overhang.

4   **5.6, 20 ft.**
    Stay to the left and avoid the overhangs.

Around the corner on the northeast (road-facing) side:

5   **5.9, 30 ft.**
    Climb the crack.

6   **5.10+, 35 ft.**
    Climb the face and the two overhangs.

## TALKING HEADWALL

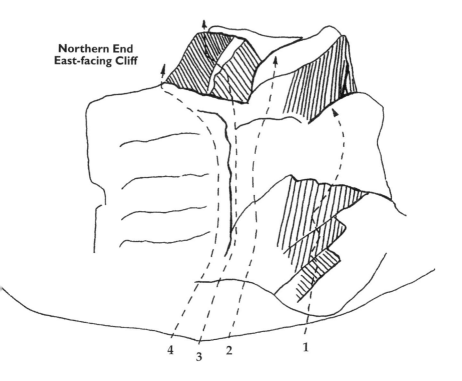

## TALKING HEADWALL

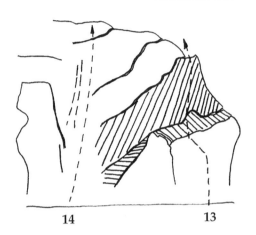

7   **5.6, 30 ft.**
    Climb the gentle overhangs below the tree on the ledge.

8   **5.6, 30 ft.**
    Climb the face beneath the tree on the ledge.

9   **5.12+, 45 ft.**
    Starting on the ramp, climb to the overhanging edge and up the largest point of the ceiling.

10  **5.12, 45 ft.**
    Climb over the edge and straight up the ceiling.

11  **5.10+, 40 ft.**
    Climb over the edge and continue up the face.

12  **5.10, 35 ft.**
    At the lowest point of the edge, climb the edge and the face above.

## TALKING HEADWALL

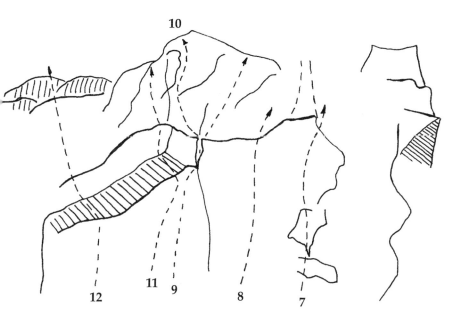

13   **5.11, 25 ft.**
     Climb the overhang.

14   **5.5, 30 ft.**
     Climb the easy face.

### NEARBY AREAS

You are close to the northern entrance of Skyline Drive at Front Royal. See the chapters dealing with Skyline Drive and Shenandoah National Park. Signal Knob, across from Massanutten Mountain, has some good routes, but these require a long approach.

### OTHER INFORMATION

Elizabeth Furnace is located in the George Washington National Forest. See Appendix B for more information on rules and regulations.

• CHAPTER 17 •

# Hone Quarry

Hone Quarry is a usually uncrowded camping area with some good top-rope and bouldering problems on a ridge top. It has a variety of beginner to intermediate climbs, with heights up to 45 feet. I often camp here when heading to other areas around the state and end up spending a lot of time on these short routes. There is also some good 10- to 12-foot scrap rock that provides good bolting or nailing practice. Like anything else in climbing, seek proper instruction from qualified instructors. You can't teach yourself new skills safely. Also, if you've never placed bolts before, don't place them in this state.

Hidden Crack is an invisible 75-foot cliff somewhere around Harrisonburg. Is it a local myth, or a cruel hoax? If you look like the workers in the local climbing stores, you can get some beta. Otherwise, you're out of luck. You'd probably have an easier time climbing the mountain in the Paramount Pictures ads.

### DIRECTIONS

From Harrisonburg, head west on Route 42 to west 257. Pass the town of Biery Branch and follow the sign to the Hone Quarry Picnic Area. From the picnic area, cross the street and follow the marked trail up the ridge top. In under a mile, you will see the cliffs. Bushwhack up to them or continue up to the ridge top and find a walk-down spot. The cliffs are listed starting at the southernmost end of the ridge top and heading north. Two other cliffs are reachable by bushwhacking up the opposite direction from the last switchback. Other areas in the Hone Quarry vicinity include scrappy 10- to 12-foot crags on the west side of the road leading from the camping area up to the lake and a 30-foot crag on the west side of the road just on the safe side of the park boundary before the picnic area.

## ROUTE DESCRIPTIONS

### HONE QUARRY

#### Area A
At the southern end of the ridge top, there are west-facing cliffs.

1. **5.10, 20 ft.**
   Go over the overhang.

2. **5.6, 20 ft.**
   Around the corner from climb 1 on the north-facing side, climb through the center of the mild overhang.

3. **5.1**
   An easy cliff face (not pictured).

4. **5.6, 15 ft.**
   Climb the leaning slab.

5. **5.6, 30 ft.**
   Layback the separating slab.

6. **5.5, 30 ft.**
   Climb the easy face to the right of the slabs.

7. **5.2, 45 ft.**
   Climb the beginner's face to the right of the overhanging blocks.

8. **5.9, 45 ft.**
   Climb over the overhanging blocks.

## HONE QUARRY

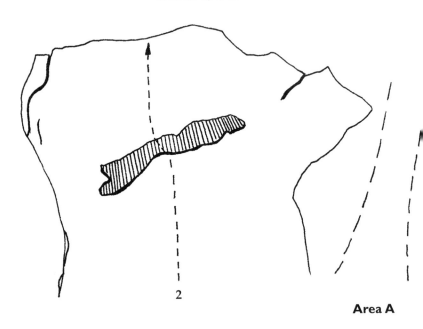

**Area A**

9  **5.8, 45 ft.**
   Climb the cracks to the left of the overhanging blocks.

10 **5.9, 30 ft.**
   Only the start is difficult. Pass over the overhang.

11 **5.10, 40 ft.**
   Another overhang.

12 **5.7, 40 ft.**
   Go through the center of the overhang.

13 **5.4–5.6 30 ft.**
   To the left of the overhangs, climb anywhere on the face.

# HONE QUARRY

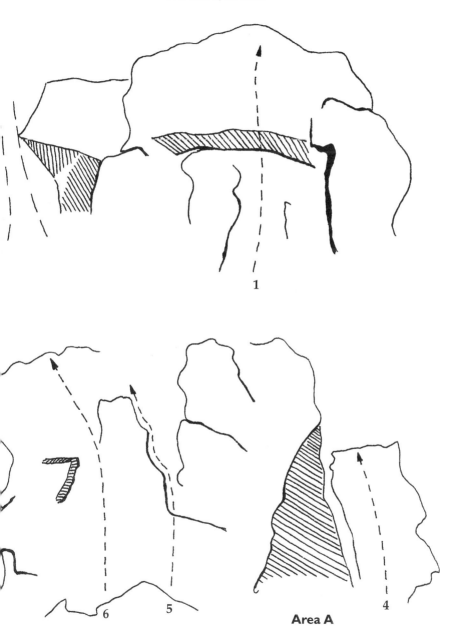

**Area A**

## HONE QUARRY

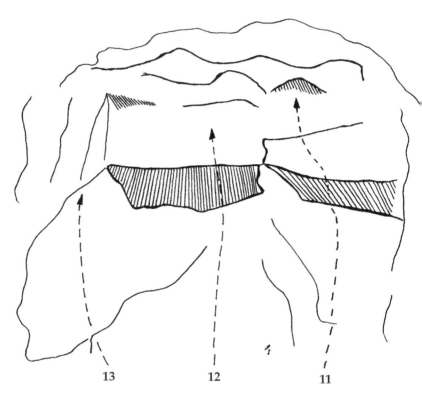

**Area A**

### Area B
These are the same cliffs, but you can find this section easily by looking for the crag with the overhangs that block the view of the top. These are also west-facing cliffs.

14   **5.12, 40 ft.**
     Climb the 5-foot roof at its widest spot.

15   **5.11, 40 ft.**
     Climb the roof at its center.

16   **5.6, 40 ft.**
     To the left of the roof, climb the cracked face.

## HONE QUARRY

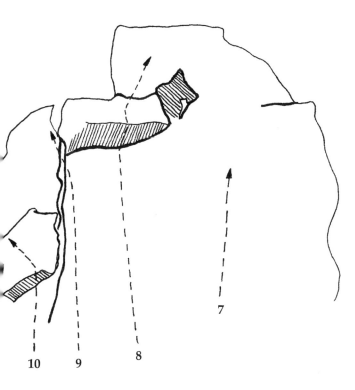

From this point on, the crag continues as scrappy 5.1–5.3 face with the usual vegetation, moss, and lichen. Several more routes are possible.

17  **5.4, 45 ft.**
    Climb anywhere on the mild face.

18  **5.1, 45 ft.**
    Easy beginner's crack to the left of climb 17.

19  **5.6, 30 ft.**
    On the south-facing outcropping, climb the face.

## HONE QUARRY

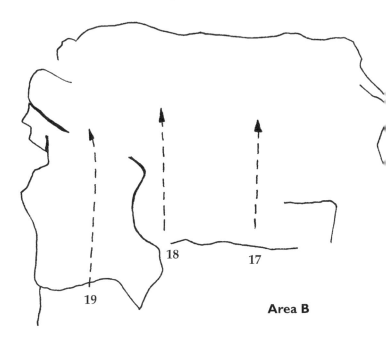

To the left of climb 19 is a good walkdown area. The trail is close—just bushwhack down about 40 yards. To the left of the walkdown is another crag (not pictured) with several 5.2 routes.

### NEARBY AREAS
Nothing is close by, but it's not far to the Blue Ridge Parkway or the Ramsey Draft Wilderness Area. Ramsey Draft has several good areas, but they are marred by very long approaches. See information on Hardscramble Knob, Bald Ridge, and Elliot Knob in Appendix A.

### OTHER INFORMATION
As stated earlier, Hone Quarry is a good camping area. The state recently started charging a $5 per site fee. Avoid paying the fee by

## HONE QUARRY

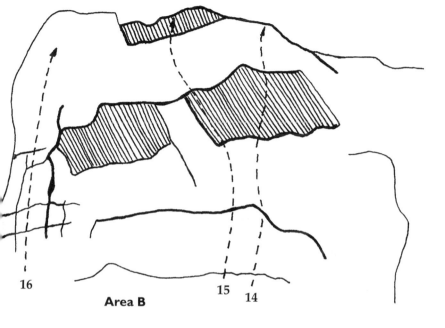

staying in a wilderness site. Check the signs for current regulations on camping areas. They have pit latrines, fresh water (the pump is closed in the winter), and clear streams. Beware of hunters in the late fall.

• CHAPTER 18 •

# Chimney Rock

This sandstone cliff is reminiscent of Seneca Rocks in West Virginia. It has several great routes on three sides but is on private property. There are a fence and "No Trespassing" signs around the cliff, and the Cootes Store sheriff is quick to appear if you even stop near the cliff. You can ask for a permit to climb here by writing to the Cootes Store VFW Post 9660. Do not climb here unless you have written permission. I do not recommend or suggest going onto private property.

### DIRECTIONS
From Route 81, take 211 west toward the town of Timberville. When you reach Timberville, turn left and head toward Broadway. Turn right onto Route 259 and go to the town of Cootes Store. The rocks are on the right.

### ROUTE DESCRIPTIONS
No specific route information is listed. If you have permission, follow the 5.8 crack on the west side to the bolts. Climbs are possible on the east, west, and south sides, but the best routes face west.

### NEARBY AREAS
There are no close areas. Heading west brings you to West Virginia, and heading east takes you to the George Washington National Forest and eventually to Shenandoah National Park.

## West Side

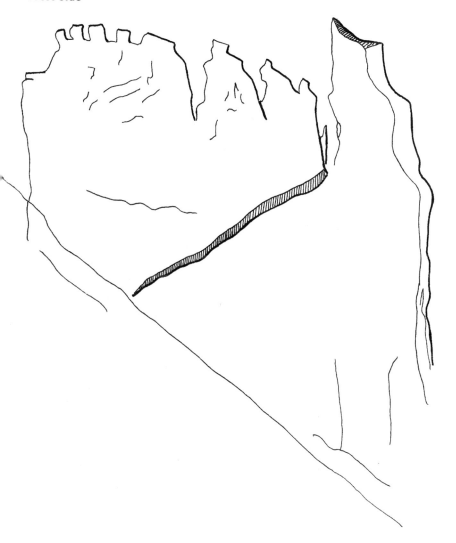

## OTHER INFORMATION
Following Route 211 east leads you to the George Washington National Forest for free camping. See Appendix B.

# · CHAPTER 19 ·

# Big Schloss, Little Schloss

It has a longer approach than most of the areas listed in this guide, but you will find great climbing on these sandstone formations. Big Schloss (Schloss is German for castle) has routes reaching 100 feet in height, including a formation with a 25-foot overhang called the Prow. Expect long, deep cracks and an assortment of pockets, micro-ledges, and shelves.

Little Schloss is an 80-foot cliff capping off a ridge top. Little Schloss has fewer routes than its bigger counterpart, but it is blessed with a shorter access, provided you have a four-wheel-drive vehicle. Little Schloss has deeper cracks and pockets than Big Schloss, but don't let this discourage you. The climbing here is excellent.

## DIRECTIONS

Reach Big Schloss from Route 81 by exiting at Edinburg. Go west on 675 away from Edinburg. Continue on 675 until you reach the Wolf Gap Camping Area. You are now almost on the West Virginia–Virginia border. Parts of Big Schloss and its surrounding trails are actually in West Virginia. Follow the trail from campsite number 9 to the ridge crest. At the first fork in the trail, stay to your left. The right fork leads to the southern summit, but the rocks there are not suitable for climbing. On the left trail, you will come to a second fork. Follow the right fork to the top of the cliffs, or follow the left trail to the base of the cliffs.

Reach Little Schloss by taking Route 81 and exiting at Edinburg. Go west on 675 away from Edinburg. Turn right onto Road 608, which turns into 88 at the "End State Maintenance" sign. Park exactly half a mile after passing Road 92. Road 92 is not marked, but someone has carved 92 into the stop sign. You are now at a fire road. With a horse, mountain bike, or jeep, you can continue up the fire road to a large field and a popular hunters' campground at the ridge top. If you're stuck with a Corolla, walk about 2 miles up the fire road. At the ridge top, follow the trail south. Little Schloss is visible in the fall, winter, or early spring, directly to the south. Several deer paths and hunter trails lead down through a small gap between the summits to the Little Schloss Cliffs.

## ROUTE DESCRIPTIONS

### BIG SCHLOSS

These routes are listed in the order you will come to them by following the cliffs along the base.

#### Area A

1. **5.8, 65 ft.**
   Follow the edge of the overhang and climb the face.

2. **5.10, 65 ft.**
   Climb through the center of the overhanging ledges.

The cliffs lose some elevation but regain it quickly. The next area is at the point where the cliff again reaches a 65- to 80-foot height. The bridge linking the rocks to the summit is also visible.

#### Area B

3. **5.9, 80 ft.**
   Follow the edge up.

4. **5.13, 80 ft.**
   Climb the overhanging ledge.

## BIG SCHLOSS

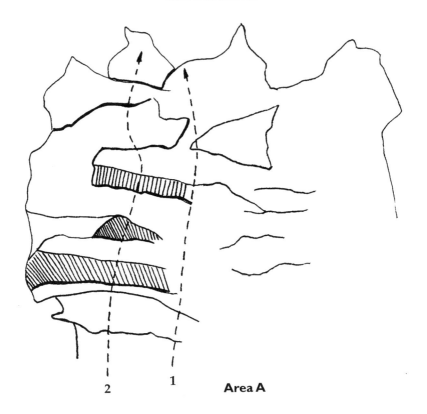

Area A

5   **5.8, 80 ft.**
Follow the easier route to the left of the large overhang.

Past the bridge on the upper cliffs is Area C.

### Area C

6   **5.9, 80 ft.**
Climb the smooth face below the ledge.

7   **5.8, 80 ft.**
Climb the face to the left of the separating slab.

## BIG SCHLOSS

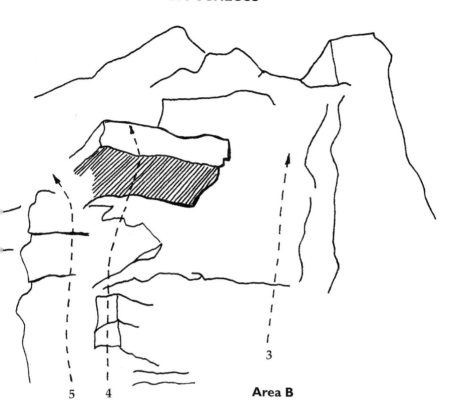

8  **5.12, 80 ft.**
   Starting below and to the right of the L-shaped cliff, climb the leaning face.

9  **5.7, 80 ft.**
   With the same start as climb number 8, follow the L-shaped crack.

There are more routes in this area, but we now move to the northernmost end. This side is distinctive due to the long overhanging formation called the Prow.

## BIG SCHLOSS

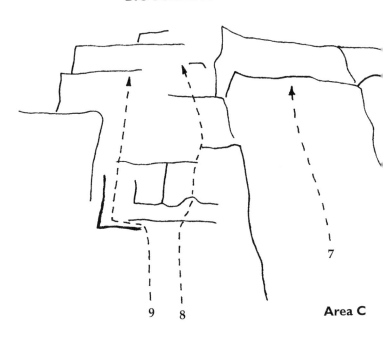

## Area D

10  **5.7, 80 ft.**
    Behind and to the right of the Prow, follow the crack and ledge system.

11  **5.?, 30 ft. high with a 25-ft. horizontal ceiling.**
    Climb straight up the Prow and out over the ceiling and up. Has this ever been finished?

12  **Prow Escape Route 5.10, 30 ft.**
    Climb the underside of the Prow, going over the short end instead of the long overhang.

Continue around the opposite side of the formation (this requires a bushwhack) to reach Area E.

# BIG SCHLOSS

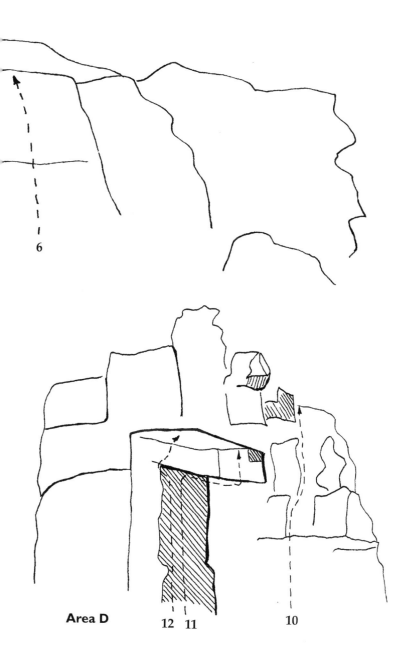

## BIG SCHLOSS

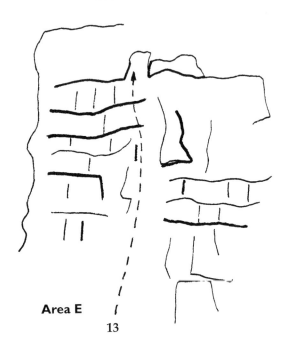

### Area E

13   **5.9, 100 ft.**
Follow the long crack system up the center of this face.

## LITTLE SCHLOSS

There are routes on both the northern and eastern sides, but only the north face is shown. The routes are listed west to east.

1   **5.9, 75 ft.**
Climb the northwestern (right) edge of the face.

2   **5.8, 75 ft.**
Around the corner from climb 1, climb the face.

## LITTLE SCHLOSS

3   **5.9, 75 ft.**
    Climb the flat face to the right of the separating slab.

4   **5.7, 80 ft.**
    Climb the off-width crack formed by the separating faces.

5   **5.10, 80 ft.**
    Climb the leaning face to the left of the deep crack.

6   **5.8, 75 ft.**
    Is this route a small chimney or a wide crack? Climb it.

7   **5.8, 50 ft.**
    On the northeastern (left) edge, climb the face.

## NEARBY AREAS

You are halfway between Seneca Rocks in West Virginia and Shenandoah National Park in Virginia. You are also in the heart of the George Washington National Forest. Check the other chapters dealing with these areas for more information.

White Rocks is another option. From Little Schloss, continue down Route 88 to where it becomes Route 713. Park and follow the Big Blue Trail up, going left at every fork until you reach White Rocks. Sometimes a gate is closed between Routes 88 and 713, making short access to White Rocks impossible.

## OTHER INFORMATION

Camp in the Wolf Gap Campground or step over into the West Virginia side and camp there. Follow all George Washington National Forest regulations. This campground, as well as many others around the state, has had some recent water contamination problems, so remember to filter or boil. Also, the national forests have recommendations about when to start fires. Please observe the rules. This is a popular area with the hunting crowd, so be especially careful in the fall and winter months.

• CHAPTER 20 •

# Clifton Forge, Low Moor (Iron Gate)

These are some of the up-and-coming areas in the state that you might be missing by driving to Seneca Rocks. Although none of them can match Seneca for history or height, the climbs are just as difficult. Clifton Forge has several sandstone cliffs up to 100 feet high. These are nice long routes overlooking the James River. The cliffs around the towns of Iron Gate and Low Moor are still in the process of being developed, so if you choose to go there, please respect the rules and do not trespass. Check access before you go. I also recommend contacting the locals and getting yourself a guide or partner. The Low Moor area has a deep cave with difficult roof problems. It also has sandstone cliffs reaching 70 feet in height.

## DIRECTIONS

Clifton Forge can be reached by leaving the town with the same name by way of Highway 220 south. The cliffs are visible from the road. Park at the historical site of the Clifton Forge for a good view. There is also a long ribbon of sandstone across the James River, but it's up to you to get over there. No route information has been included for the Clifton Forge area.

Low Moor is reachable by getting off Highway 64 at the town of Low Moor and going west on Route 1101. Turn left onto Road 1102. Go to the end and turn right onto 1104. The areas are on the right.

## ROUTE DESCRIPTIONS

### LOW MOOR

Facing the cave entrance:

1. **5.10+, 70 ft.**
   To the left of the cave entrance, climb the face.

2. **5.12, 70 ft.**
   Climb up to the center of the cave mouth and climb the upper face.

3. **5.9, 70 ft.**
   To the right of the cave entrance, climb the face.

In the cave on the right side:

4. **5.6, 25 ft.**
   Close to the entrance of the cave, climb the cave side.

5. **5.9, 20 ft.**
   Toward the rear of the cave, climb the cave side.

In the cave on the left side:

6. **5.12+, 22 ft.**
   Climb the roof.

Outside the cave, heading east, back toward I-64:

7. **5.10, 70 ft.**
   Climb the difficult crack to the series of overhanging blocks.

8. **5.9, 70 ft.**
   Climb the crack, but stay to the right of the overhangs.

9. **5.7, 70 ft.**
   Climb the face over the ledges.

10. **5.6, 70 ft.**
    Take the easy route away from the leaning faces.

The cliff continues with a variety of routes ranging from 5.6 to 5.9. There are also some cliffs up on the ridge and in the center of the highway. Avoid the highway.

## LOW MOOR

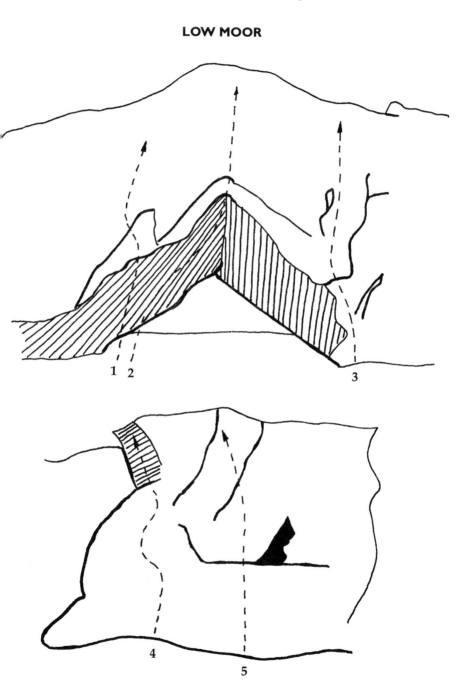

## LOW MOOR

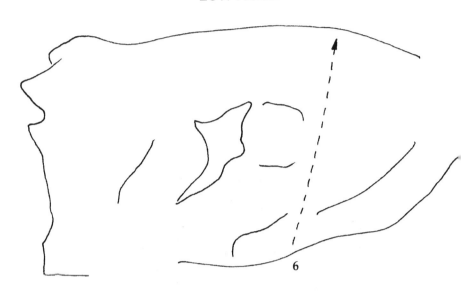

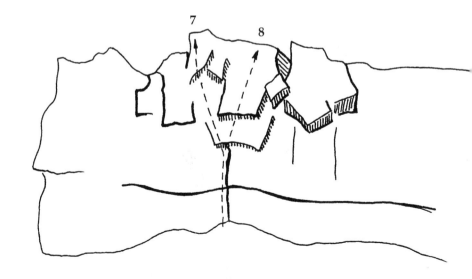

## LOW MOOR

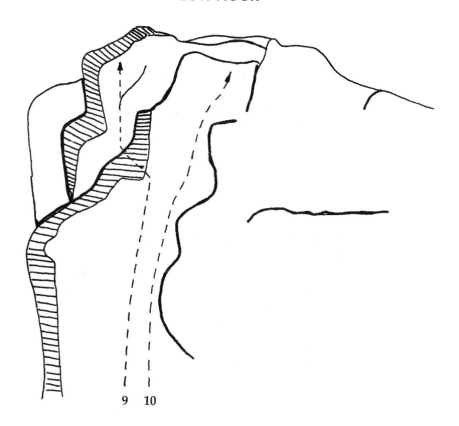

### NEARBY AREAS
All the climbs around the Roanoke area are nearby. See Chapter 23.
  Covington Cliffs is rumored to be visible from I-64. I've never seen it despite the fact that the cliffs are supposed to be over 100 feet tall. Maybe they are a mirage of Seneca.

### OTHER INFORMATION
You are in the George Washington National Forest and very close to the Jefferson National Forest. Camp anywhere, or try Douthat State Park, just north of the town of Clifton Forge. See Appendix B for more information on the national forest system.

# CHAPTER 21

# Crabtree Falls, Pedlar District

Crabtree Falls is the highest waterfall east of the Mississippi and cascades over 1,080 feet in five vertical sections, the largest being 500 feet. If this looks familiar, you probably saw it on the old TV show "The Waltons." The trail up to the falls offers three large cliffs with heights up to 50 feet. It has a few tough ceiling problems and a variety of challenging boulder problems. None of the cliffs that make up the falls are listed. Depending on the wetness of the season and the height of the Tye River, the falls might be climbable, but many people have died because they misjudged the slipperiness of the rocks close to the falls. For this reason, you should stick to the climbs listed here and avoid the cliffs that make up the falls. Ice climbing is another possibility here, but only in the most severe winters.

## DIRECTIONS

Take Route 81 south about 20 miles past Staunton to Exit 205. Go toward Steel Tavern. Take Route 56 east to the Crabtree Falls parking lot. The parking lot is 13.5 miles from Route 81 or 6.6 miles from the Blue Ridge Parkway Tye River Gap exit. The furthest rocks listed here are an easy 1.4 miles from the parking lot. The cliffs are listed in the order that you will come to them.

## ROUTE DESCRIPTIONS

### AREA A

#### Northeast Face

1. **The Blocks 5.3, 35 ft.**
   On the far right side of the cliff, climb the terrace blocks.

2. **5.6, 45 ft.**
   Climb the crack on the right flake. Variation: Start a traverse here at the horizontal crack level and proceed over to climb 10 and around the corner.

3. **5.9, 50 ft.**
   Climb the smooth face to the right of the horizontal crack.

4. **5.9, 50 ft.**
   Climb the smooth face to the right of the large flake.

5. **5.10, 50 ft.**
   Climb the right underhang of the large flake.

6. **5.10, 50 ft.**
   Climb the center of the large flake.

7. **5.8, 50 ft.**
   Climb the face to the left of the large flake. Variation: Climb the 5.5 crack on the left of the large flake.

8. **5.4, 50 ft.**
   To the right of the first crack, climb the easy layback.

9. **5.6, 50 ft.**
   Near the left edge, climb the first crack.

10. **5.10, 48 ft.**
    Near the left edge, climb the leaning face to the left of the first crack.

## CRABTREE FALLS

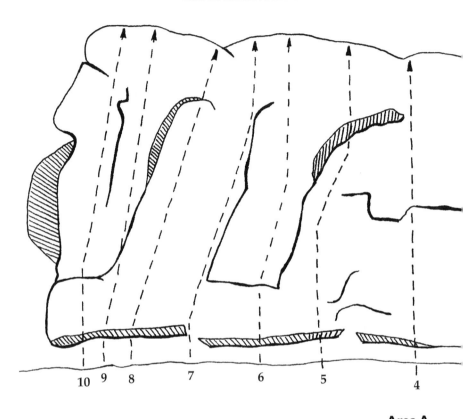

Area A

**East Face**

11  **5.5, 40 ft.**
    Climb the easy cracks anywhere on the right edge.

12  **5.5, 40 ft.**
    Climb the center of the downward flakes.

13  **5.6, 40 ft.**
    Climb the left edge of the downward flake. Use layback techniques.

## CRABTREE FALLS

**Northeast Face**

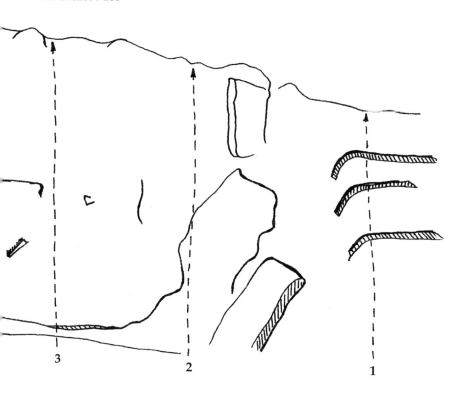

**14** **5.6, 40 ft.**
Climb the face without using the crack on the left.

**15** **5.5, 40 ft.**
Climb the right side of the slight outcropping.

**16** **5.5, 30 ft.**
On the left of the outcrop, climb the face.

**17** **5.8, 25 ft.**
Climb the center of the 4-foot overhang.

## CRABTREE FALLS

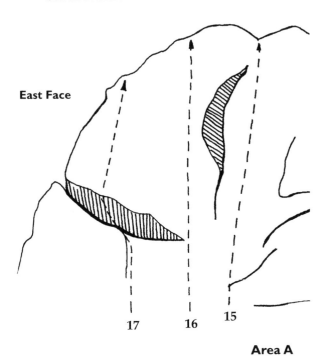

**Area A**

---

### AREA B

18  5.11-, 12 ft.
Climb the northwest-facing leaning block.

---

### AREA C

**North Face**

19  Good bouldering area.

20  5.9, 15 ft.
In between the large cracks, climb the leaning face.

21  5.7, 18 ft.
To the left of the large crack, climb the leaning face.

# CRABTREE FALLS

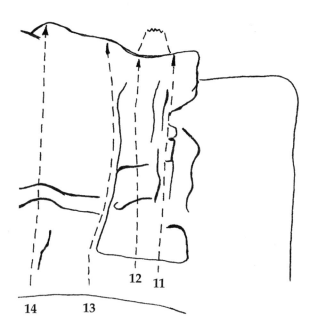

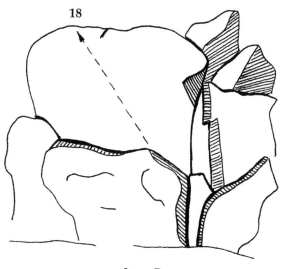

**Area B**

## CRABTREE FALLS

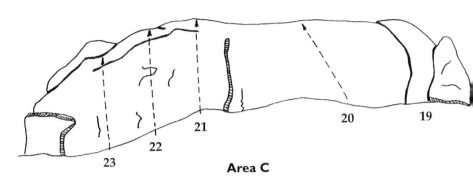

Area C

22  5.8, 20 ft.
    Beneath the slight flake, climb the leaning face.

23  Easy beginner climbs on the left end of this cliff.

## AREA D

24  18 ft.
    North-facing beginner face with smooth holds covered with moss.

## AREA E

### Northeast Face

25  5.11, 22 ft.
    Climb the right boulder onto the suspended block.

26  **Chimneys 5.3–5.4, 30 ft.**
    Under the suspended block, three good chimney problems exist. The two chimneys on the left lead to the inner walls of the southeast face.

27  5.13, 20 ft.
    On the back wall under the suspended block, climb across the ceiling and up over the block. Since this block can be climbed on three different sides, many variations are possible.

# CRABTREE FALLS

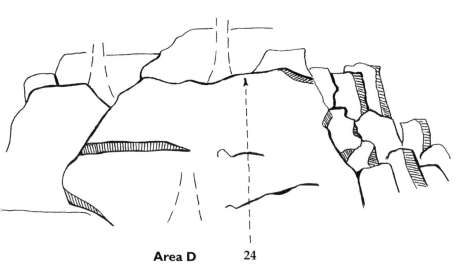

Area D   24

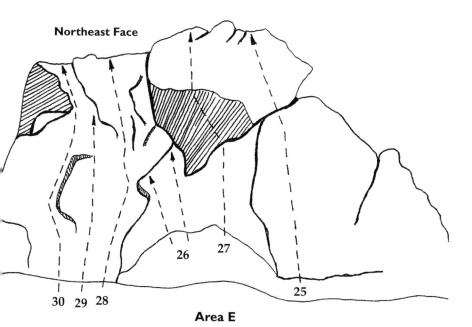

Northeast Face

30  29  28     26  27         25

Area E

**28** **5.3, 20 ft.**
On the left of the block, climb the easy ledge.

**29** **5.6, 20 ft.**
Climb the face to the left of the suspended block.

**30** **5.5, 20 ft.**
Climb to the left of the C-shaped scar.

### East Face

**31** **Easy Crack 5.2, 18 ft.**
Around the corner of climbs 28–30, climb anywhere on the moss-covered face.

**CRABTREE FALLS**

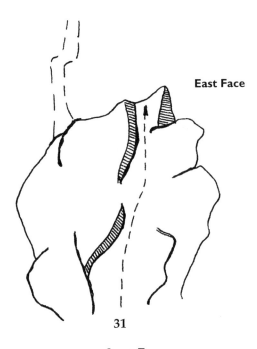

**Area E**

## Southeast Face

**32**    **5.2, 12 ft.**
Around the corner of climb 31, climb the easy face.

**33**    **5.5, 14 ft.**
On left side of the large opening, climb the face with the slight overhanging bulge.

## Inner Faces

These are entered through the large opening between climbs 32 and 33 or by chimney 26.

**34**    **5.7, 30 ft.**
On the wall closest to the suspended block, climb the leaning face to the right of the overhang.

**35**    **5.10, 30 ft.**
On the wall closest to the suspended block, climb the leaning face through the overhang.

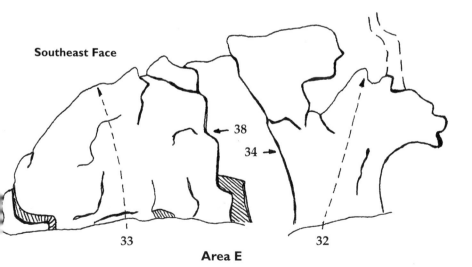

**CRABTREE FALLS**

Area E

## CRABTREE FALLS

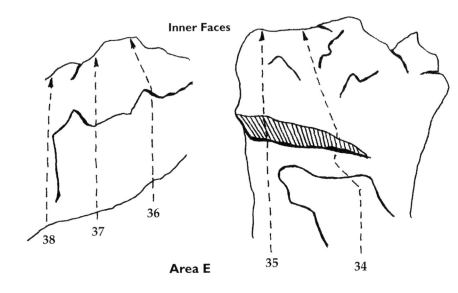

36 **5.9, 25 ft.**
On the opposite wall of climbs 34 and 35, climb the inner edge.

37 **5.7, 25 ft.**
As above, but stay to the left of climb 36 and to the right of the crack.

38 **5.7, 25 ft.**
As in climb 36, but follow the crack up.

### NEARBY AREAS

There is much climbing along the nearby Blue Ridge Parkway. See Chapter 22. The Pedlar district is virtually untapped when it comes to climbing. In the Pedlar district, try these areas: Mine Bank, St. Mary's River Cliffs, Cellar Mountain, Mills Creek (bouldering), Campbell Creek Canyon, Panther Falls, Staton's Falls, and Indian Rocks. They have not been included due to space limitations and because many of them are small and require at least a 5-mile hike. A good trail guide can direct you to these areas.

## OTHER INFORMATION

Crabtree Falls has ample parking and pit toilets, but it has no camping. See Chapters 28 and 30 for nearby camping options or continue up the trail (2.9 miles from the parking lot) to Crabtree Falls Meadows for free camping.

• CHAPTER 22 •

# Ravens Roost, Love Gap, White Rocks, Twenty-Minute Cliff, Humpback Rock

Here are some great climbs right along the Blue Ridge Parkway. For the most part, you'll be parking at the top of the crag.

Raven's Roost has always been a popular area with local climbers, and there are usually several small groups there on the weekends. During the week, you'll probably have this area to yourself. It also serves as a take-off point for hang gliders. Expect cliffs up to 80 feet in height.

Love Gap also has cliffs up to 80 feet in height, but check on access before hitting this crag. Love Gap is not pictured.

White Rocks Cliff has some good routes up to 70 feet. There are no trails that reach this crag, so head to them only if you're good at bushwhacking. Trail guides to the Pedlar district might show some trails that can bring you to White Rocks faster than the parkway. White Rocks Cliff is not pictured.

Twenty-Minute Cliff offers some good routes up to 30 feet. Early farmers in the White Rock Valley area named the cliff when they realized that during corn-chopping season, twenty minutes after sunlight hit the cliff face, dusk would fall on the valley.

Humpback Rock sees some climbing traffic, but I can't imagine why. The designers of this trail never considered switchbacks, but instead placed benches along the trail. I suspect Humpback Rock is the site of many heart attacks among the out-of-shape tourists and senior citizens heading up the trail. Leave this area to the tourists and head to Raven's Roost. The rocks at Humpback Rock are not pictured.

## DIRECTIONS

Reach these areas by driving south from Rockfish Gap. Rockfish Gap is the northern end of the Blue Ridge Parkway and is just south of the town of Waynesboro.

The Humpback Rock parking area is at mile marker 6. Park at the Visitor Center and head up the marked trail. There are some cliffs before you reach the rocks at the summit. Raven's Roost has a small parking area at mile marker 10.7. The cliffs are directly below the parking spaces. Love Gap is at mile marker 16 on the east side of the parkway. White Rocks Cliffs are visible down in the valley at mile marker 19.5. Twenty-Minute Cliff is found at mile marker 19. Park at the overlook, because the cliff is directly below.

## ROUTE DESCRIPTIONS

### RAVEN'S ROOST

It is possible to walk down from either end, but the south end is the faster choice.

#### Area A

1. **Total Control 5.13, 45 ft.**
   Climb the north leaning face.

### RAVEN'S ROOST LAYOUT

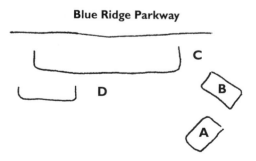

# RAVEN'S ROOST

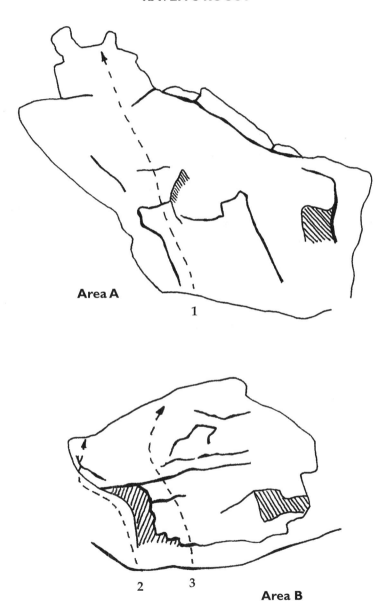

Area A

Area B

## Area B

2. **5.10, 15 ft.**
   Climb the overhang on the northwest edge.

3. **5.9, 25 ft.**
   Climb the center of the north side.

## Area C

Climbs 4 through 7 are on the south end of the cliff.

4. **5.6, 40 ft.**
   At the far western end of the crag, climb the face.

5. **5.10, 45 ft.**
   Climb anywhere on the face to the left of the L-shaped impression.

6. **5.9, 40 ft.**
   Climb the face to the left of the horizontal crack.

7. **5.9, 30 ft.**
   To the right of the crack, climb the face, avoiding the crack edge.

8. **5.7, 30 ft.**
   Climb the off-width crack.

## Area D

Climbs are on the west face.

9. **5.8, 50 ft.**
   Climb the face around the corner from climb 8.

10. **5.9, 55 ft.**
    Climb the face.

11. **5.7, 55 ft.**
    Climb the crack.

12. **5.8, 70 ft.**
    To the left of the crack, climb anywhere on the face. Several different 5.8 variations are possible.

# RAVEN'S ROOST

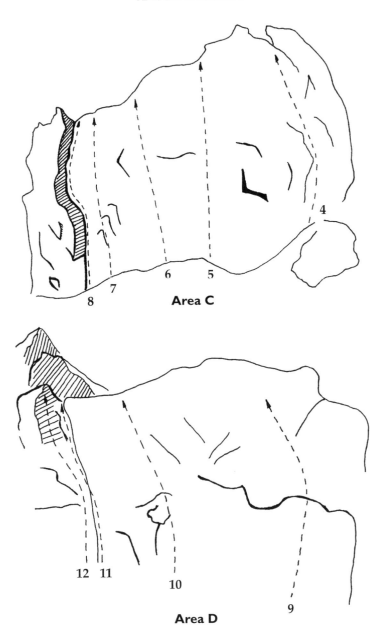

Area C

Area D

13  **5.8, 60 ft.**
Climb the slab edges.

14  **5.8, 65 ft.**
Climb the face.

15  **5.7, 70 ft.**
Climb the face on the right side of the ledge.

16  **5.5, 60 ft.**
Climb the face through the center of the outcropping.

17  **5.8, 40 ft.**
Climb the leaning ramp.

18  **5.6, 40 ft.**
Climb the center of the outcropping that forms the ramp.

19  **5.5, 45 ft.**
To the left of the ramp, follow the edge.

20  **5.6, 70 ft.**
Climb the center of the face.

21  **5.4, 70 ft.**
Follow the easy ledges.

22  **5.3, 70 ft.**
Climb the easy face to the crack.

23  **5.5, 75 ft.**
Starting at the center of the ledges, climb the face.

24  **5.5, 55 ft.**
When the cliff lowers to a height of 55 feet and trees crop up on the lower ledges, climb anywhere on the face.

From this point on, the cliff becomes a lichen-covered Grade IV cliff. One 5.6 route (not pictured) has been done. The far east end of Area D again reaches a height of 55 feet and has some routes ranging from 5.3 to 5.5 (not pictured).

## RAVEN'S ROOST

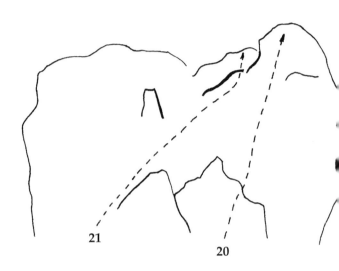

Area D

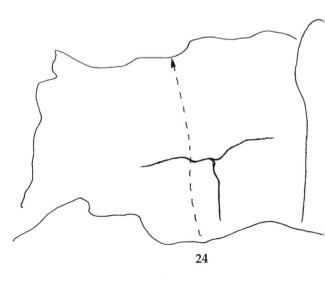

## RAVEN'S ROOST

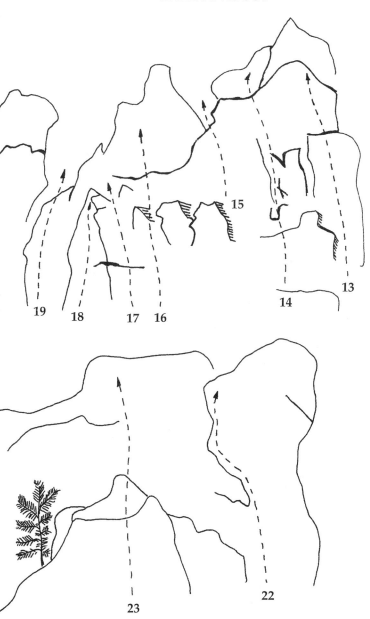

## TWENTY-MINUTE CLIFF

The easiest walkdown is on the north side of the parking area.
Detached boulder—west-facing side:

**1  5.6, 18 ft.**
Toward the southwest end, climb the boulder.

**2  5.10, 18 ft.**
In the center of the detached boulder, climb the face.

Main cliff—west-facing, starting from the north end.

**3  5.4, 30 ft.**
To the left of the walkdown, climb the face.

### TWENTY-MINUTE CLIFF

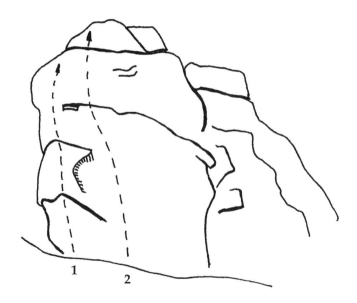

**Detached Boulder
West-facing Side**

## TWENTY-MINUTE CLIFF

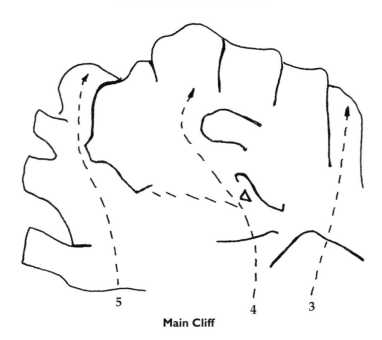

Main Cliff

4   **5.4, 30 ft.**
    Avoid the ledges and head diagonally up.

5   **5.7, 30 ft.**
    Climb the face.

6   **5.9, 30 ft.**
    Climb the leaning ledges.

7   **5.8, 30 ft.**
    To the right of the S-shaped scars, climb the face past the outcrops.

8   **5.8, 30 ft.**
    Climb the face through the center of the S-shaped scars.

## TWENTY-MINUTE CLIFF

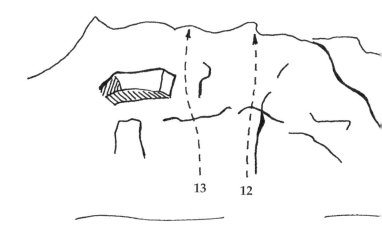

Main Cliff

9   **5.6, 30 ft.**
    To the left of the S-shaped scar, climb the center of the face.

10  **5.5, 30 ft.**
    Climb over the outcrops to the right of the leaning block.

11  **5.7, 30 ft.**
    Climb through the center of the leaning block.

12  **5.4, 30 ft.**
    Climb the easy face to the right of the long crack.

13  **5.6, 30 ft.**
    Climb the face at the southernmost end of Twenty-Minute Cliff.

## TWENTY-MINUTE CLIFF

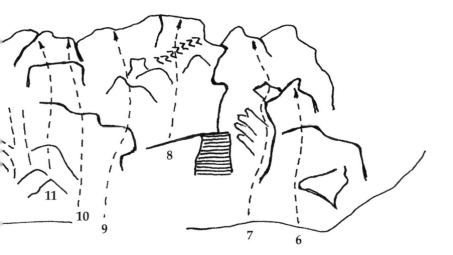

### NEARBY AREAS

You can try Rock Point, which is reachable from the Rock Point Overlook at mile marker 10.4. Rock Point has 20 foot boulders that are overgrown and boring.

Big Spy Mountain is visible from the Blue Ridge Parkway at mile marker 26.3. From what I can see, it's a 3,185 foot peak covered with greenstone. It's located in the park, but no roads or trails are shown on the maps.

### OTHER INFORMATION

All Blue Ridge Parkway regulations are in effect. See Appendix B.

• CHAPTER 23 •

# McAfee's Knob, Dragon's Tooth, Eagle Rock

These areas are close to Roanoke. McAfee's Knob offers some excellent climbing routes along the Appalachian Trail near Catawba Mountain. These sandstone routes range from 20 to 30 feet in height with all levels of difficulty. This area sees much traffic from the crowd around Roanoke. The routes are obvious, but if you need route name information, check at the local climbing stores.

Dragon's Tooth has 100-foot sandstone cliffs only a short hike down the Appalachian Trail. The climbs are great, although the routes are rarely higher than 60 feet.

The town of Eagle Rock, located north of Roanoke, has several sandstone cliffs up to 100 feet in height. The climbs are short and the area is in the early stages of development. Although it is not a wonderful area, it does have a couple of nice routes. There are two abandoned quarries in the town of Eagle Rock. No matter how tempting it may seem, do not climb in the quarries. They are on private property and are marked with "No Trespassing" signs.

### DIRECTIONS

**McAfee's Knob.** Reach the knob from Roanoke by driving north on Highway 311. Park at the Appalachian Trailhead marker on the left about 10 miles from Roanoke. The trail leads both north and south, so make sure you go north. Hike up the trail, and you will come to the top of the cliffs. Be careful of trail descriptions in this area; the trail has moved, changed, and been renamed over the years.

**Dragon's Tooth.** Reach Dragon's Tooth by taking Route 311 north out of Roanoke. Park on the left when you see the Dragon's Tooth sign, just after passing Route 624. The road up has been torn out as of this printing, which makes for a longer hike. Go south on the Appalachian Trail 2.5 miles to the area. No routes at Dragon's Tooth are pictured.

**Eagle Rock.** Take Route 220 north toward the town of Eagle Rock. Cross the bridge over the James River for a cliff group by the road. I avoid climbing close to the road, but I have heard that there are some good routes up above on the ridge. Park in the Veterans' Picnic Area.

**EAGLE ROCK AREAS**

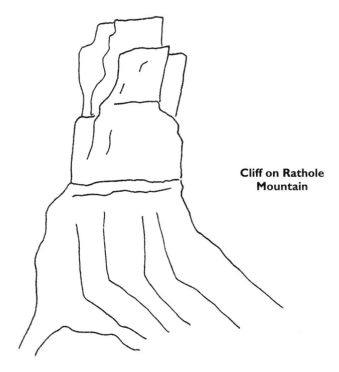

**Cliff on Rathole Mountain**

## EAGLE ROCK AREAS

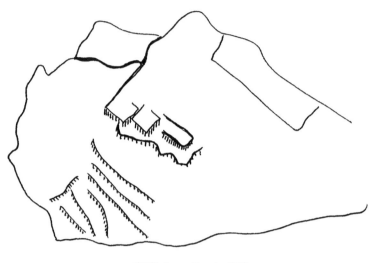

**Cliff along Route 220**

The main area at Eagle Rock is back across the bridge. This large cliff on Rathole Mountain (I didn't make it up) has a large ledge. On the south side of the cliff, take the steep path up to the graffiti-covered ledge. The routes are on this upper face.

### ROUTE DESCRIPTIONS

#### MCAFEE'S KNOB

The climbs are listed from the northernmost end back down the ridge.

1. **5.9, 20 ft.**
   Climb the face.

2. **5.9, 20 ft.**
   Climb the leaning face.

3. **5.2, 20 ft.**
   Climb the easy face.

## MCAFEE'S KNOB

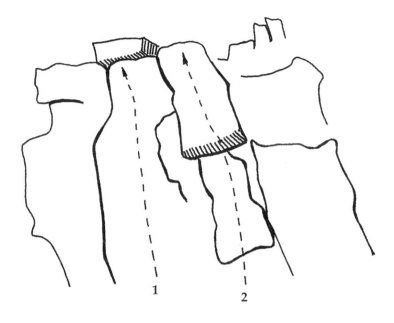

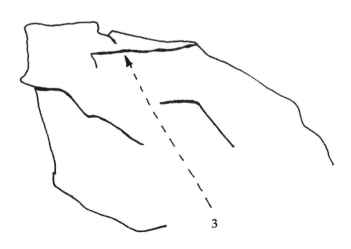

## MCAFEE'S KNOB

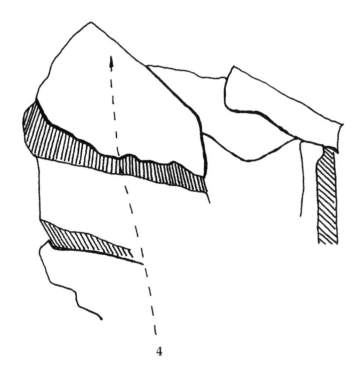

4

4   **5.10, 20 ft.**
    Climb the leaning face past two overhangs.

On the next grouping of routes:

5   **5.6, 20 ft.**
    Climb anywhere on the pock-marked face.

6   **5.4, 20 ft.**
    Climb toward the left edge of the face.

7   **5.8, 20 ft.**
    Climb the center.

## MCAFEE'S KNOB

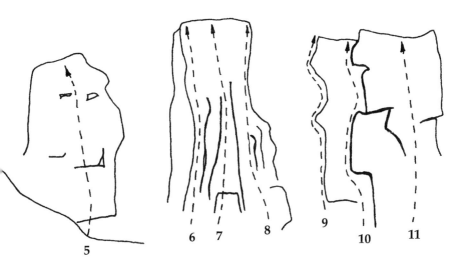

8   **5.5, 20 ft.**
    Climb the right edge.

   Around the corner:

9   **5.6, 20 ft.**
    Climb the edge formed by the corner.

10  **5.6, 20 ft.**
    Follow the edge created by the flake.

11  **5.4, 20 ft.**
    Climb anywhere on the easy face.

## MCAFEE'S KNOB

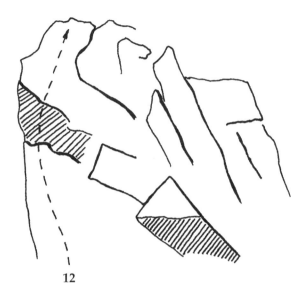

12

Further down:

**12  5.9, 22 ft.**
Climb the face.

Still further down at section called the Kitchen or Hell's Kitchen:

**13  5.11, 20 ft.**
Climb over the 10-foot roof.

**14  5.9, 20 ft.**
Avoid the overhangs by climbing around the ledge to the left.

**15  5.12+, 20 ft.**
Climb the leaning face and the 15-foot roof.

**16  5.5, 18 ft.**
Starting at the far right end, climb the face to the right of the roof.

## HELL'S KITCHEN

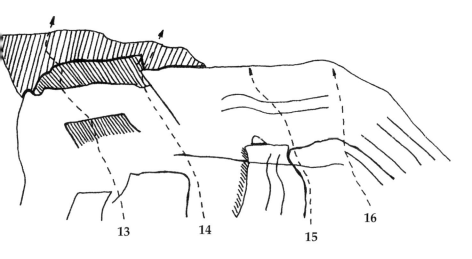

There are many other bouldering options around. Two nice boulders are on the Catawba Fire Road. From McAfee's Knob, head down to the parking area via the Catawba Fire Road. The boulders are on the left side next to the road.

17  **5.7, 15 ft.**
    Climb the cracked ledge.

18  **5.10+, 18 ft.**
    Climb the leaning face.

19  **5.9, 18 ft.**
    Starting at the short rows of vertical cracks, climb the face.

20  **5.9, 18 ft.**
    Climb the edge around and up by starting to the right of climb 19.

## CATAWBA FIRE ROAD BOULDERS

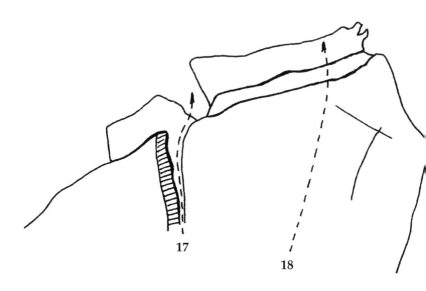

**21  5.5, 15 ft.**
Around the corner, climb the easy face.

### NEARBY AREAS

It is not far to Iron Gate or Clifton Forge. It is also a short distance to Seneca Rocks, one of the greatest (but most crowded) areas on the East Coast. Stick to the Virginia areas, and you will do more climbing and less waiting.

Fenwick Mines has some formations after a short hike. From New Castle (north of Roanoke), take Route 615 and turn left onto Barbours Creek Road. After a quarter of a mile, turn right onto 685, which leads to 181 and the Fenwick Mines Parking Area. Follow the marked (and paved) trails.

## CATAWBA FIRE ROAD BOULDERS

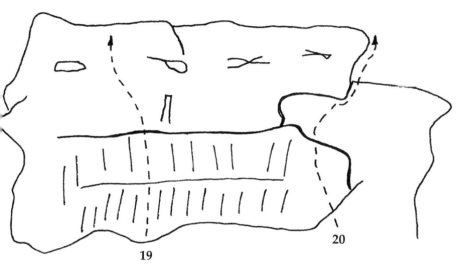

## OTHER INFORMATION
You will find good camping south of Eagle Rock at North Creek or Colon Hollow. Both are in the Jefferson National Forest. There is also good camping to the north of Clifton Forge at Douthat State Park.

# PART V

# Thomas Jefferson National Forest

# · CHAPTER 24 ·

# White Face, Fool's Face

These two sandstone cliffs are located near Blacksburg. They face each other across the New River. White Face reaches heights of 145 feet, and its sister cliff is just under 45 feet tall. Avoid the railroad property, and you can have a good time on these cliffs. After climbing, cool off with a jump into the New River.

## DIRECTIONS

**White Face.** Leave Blacksburg on Highway 114. Turn right onto Route 600 and drive to the end. Hike up the steep trail to the cliffs.

**Fool's Face.** Leave Blacksburg and take Prices Fork Road (Route 685, which becomes Route 652) until you reach the town of McCoy Falls. The cliffs are by the railroad tracks. Make every effort to avoid the tracks. Virginia has a $50 fine for trespassing (walking) along the railroad tracks. There is also a parking area.

## NEARBY AREAS

There are no great areas nearby, but the Blacksburg climbing stores might give you some suggestions.

## OTHER INFORMATION

Camp anywhere around the Thomas Jefferson National Forest. Developed campgrounds north of Blacksburg include Caldwell Fields and White Rocks. Claytor Lake State Park is south of Blacksburg and Radford.

# Wytheville Cliff (Marion Cliff)

Here's a good case of false advertising. The 120-foot-tall Wytheville Cliff is actually located in the town of Marion. This is also a case of access ruining an area. Please check the access issues before climbing here and respect any changes regarding access to the area. The last time I climbed here, the landowners did not mind climbers but did not allow any parking near the cliff or on the road reaching the cliff. Likewise, all the businesses for miles around the area did not allow parking. My solution was to take a long bike ride to the cliff from a distant parking area.

### DIRECTIONS

Reach Marion Cliff by taking Route 11 through Marion and turning right on Johnston Road. Continue on Johnston Road past the railroad tracks. The cliffs are directly on the right and face west.

### ROUTE DESCRIPTIONS

1. **5.9, 120 ft.**
   Climb the long crack by the outcropping edge.

2. **5.10, 120 ft.**
   Climb the large leaning face.

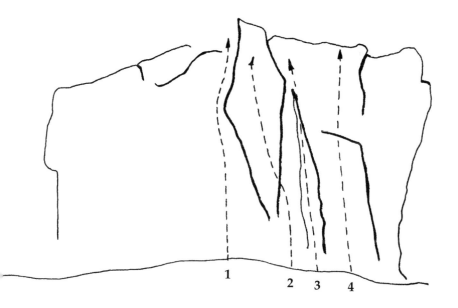

**3  5.7, 120 ft.**
To the right of the leaning face, climb the long crack.

**4  5.10, 120 ft.**
On the southernmost end, climb the tough face.

## NEARBY AREAS

Head south to Grayson Highlands State Park or to the Little Stoney Creek Cliffs at the Hanging Rock Picnic Area. See Chapters 26 and 27.

## OTHER INFORMATION

Go north on Route 16 out of Marion to reach the Hungry Mother State Park for camping. Alternatively, you can head south out of Marion and camp anywhere in the Thomas Jefferson National Forest. See Appendix B for national forest regulations.

# CHAPTER 26

# Little Stoney Creek Cliffs

Little Stoney Creek Cliffs are located near the entrance to the Hanging Rock Picnic Area. This is a small area with a very short access and nice routes up to 65 feet. If you are in the area, take a look.

## DIRECTIONS

From the town of Coeburn, go 7.5 miles south on Route 72 to the Hanging Rock Picnic Area. The crag pictured is by the first pull-off before the gate and is across the stream. There are more cliffs in the area. They are visible up the ridge and can be reached from the various trails that intersect in the picnic area. Trailheads in the picnic area can guide you to more cliffs. These trails are long, so be prepared for a 5- to 8-mile hike. There are two waterfalls that cascade a distance of 70 feet. They freeze solid, but are they worth the hike? The front gate is locked and the water is shut off after Labor Day. Don't let the gate discourage you; the trails are still accessible, and the crag pictured is outside the gate.

## ROUTE DESCRIPTIONS

On the south-facing side:

1. **5.5, 50 ft.**
   Climb the face.

2. **5.7, 60 ft.**
   Climb the overhang.

3. **5.8, 65 ft.**
   To the right of scars, climb the face.

On the southeast-facing side:

4. **5.9, 65 ft.**
   Climb the leaning face.

## LITTLE STONEY CREEK CLIFFS

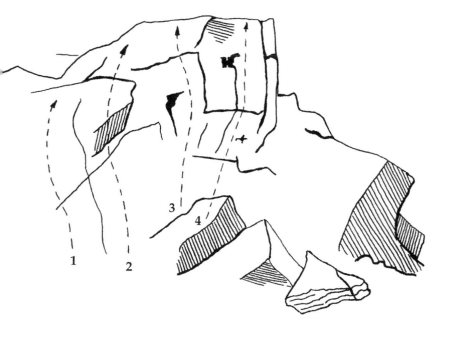

## LITTLE STONEY CREEK CLIFFS

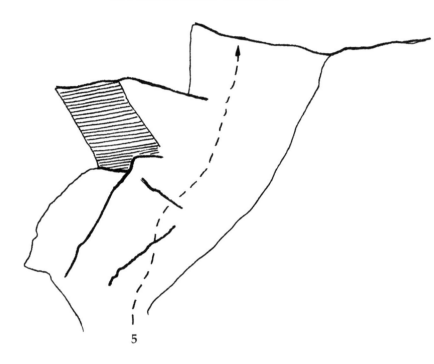

On the east-facing side:

5   **5.5, 65+ft.**
    Follow the rib up the hillside.

### NEARBY AREAS
Since you are in the area, check out Listening Rock in the heart of Grayson Highlands State Park.

### OTHER INFORMATION
Follow the regulations of the Thomas Jefferson National Forest. See Appendix B for information on camping in the national forest.

# PART VI

# State Parks and Miscellaneous Areas

## • CHAPTER 27 •

# Grayson Highlands

Grayson Highlands State Park has a variety of small areas with easy access. The best area is Buzzard Rock. (Every state has two or three Buzzard Rocks. You'd think they could be more original.) This Buzzard Rock is also called Listening Rock. Expect intermediate and advanced routes up to 45 feet in height. Be careful, because not much climbing has been done in this area, and much of the rock is still loose.

Other climbing areas in the park include Big Pinnacle, Little Pinnacle, Twin Pinnacle, and Massies Gap Overlook. The view from Massies Gap Overlook shows areas of Kentucky, Tennessee, and Virginia. The climbing at these areas is only average, but there are some nice bouldering problems. I have not listed or pictured any of these areas. To reach them, go to either the parking area or the visitors' center and follow the trail markers.

### DIRECTIONS

You can reach Grayson Highlands Park by taking Route 81 south to the town of Marion. Take Route 16 southeast and follow signs to Grayson Highlands State Park. Reach Buzzard Rock or Listening Rock by parking at the visitors' center and following the Buzzard Rock Trail.

## ROUTE DESCRIPTIONS

Along the Buzzard Rock Trail, the crags and climbs appear in the order that you will come across them.

1. **5.7, 15 ft.**
   Climb the overhang on the northwest-facing boulder.

2. **5.8, 15 ft.**
   On the right end, climb the sloping face.

Further down the path on the north face:

3. **5.3, 20 ft.**
   Climb the crack.

4. **5.6, 20 ft.**
   Climb the center of this small crag.

5. **5.3, 20 ft.**
   Climb the face to the left of the lichen-covered wall.

Buzzard or Listening Rock can be reached at the end of the Buzzard Rock Trail. Rock steps lead you to the top of the cliffs. Check out the view, then backtrack down the steps and head to the cliff base. The cliff faces north.

6. **5.8, 45 ft.**
   Climb the cracked leaning face.

7. **5.9, 45 ft.**
   To the left of the smooth face, climb the leaning face.

8. **5.10, 45 ft.**
   Climb the smooth face.

9. **5.12, 40 ft.**
   Climb the blocky outcropping.

10. **5.6–5.9, 40 ft.**
    Too much loose rock?

11. **5.9, 35 ft.**
    Climb the leaning face.

## Rocks along Buzzard Rock Trail

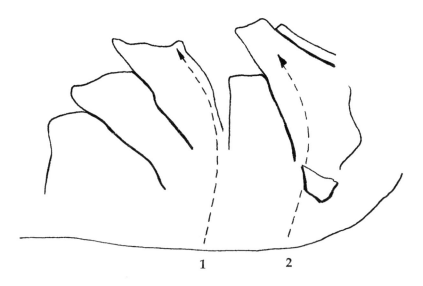

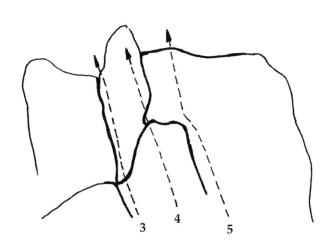

## Listening Rock

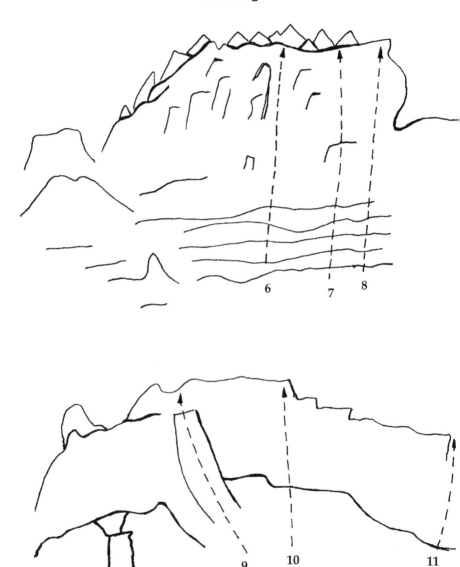

## NEARBY AREAS

There is nothing close by, but you can drive north to the town of Marion or over to the Hanging Rock Picnic Area for the Little Stoney Creek Cliffs.

## OTHER INFORMATION

Good camping is available in Grayson Highlands State Park. See Appendix B for information on camping in the state parks. Keep an eye open for wild horses.

## CHAPTER 28

# Moorman's Boulders

Moorman's Boulders is a little climbing area near Charlottesville with a great selection of short routes of all grades. The tallest cliff reaches almost 30 feet. Although this area has been used for years, the locals are still skittish about outsiders. This area has been mentioned in several guidebooks. Information on Moorman's Boulders occasionally appears on the Internet. Despite all this, hordes of outsiders have not appeared, nor have they impacted the area. If you decide to climb in this area, respect the local customs.

I have not included any route names for this area, because permission was not given. All the routes are well chalked. Note to locals: Pick up some of the tape balls, carpet squares, and other trash. A clean area will stay clean, because people will respect it.

### DIRECTIONS

From Charlottesville, take Barracks Road 12 miles and turn right on Route 671. (Barracks Road becomes Garth Road a few miles past the city limits.) Go toward the town of Millington. In under 2 miles, you will see a short trestle bridge. The cliffs are visible on the right from the road. Park along the road. Do not block the entrances to any properties.

## ROUTE DESCRIPTIONS

On the west (road)-facing side:

1. **5.9, 20 ft.**
   Climb the face and the overhang.

2. **5.6, 20 ft.**
   Climb the face to the right of the overhang.

3. **5.9, 20 ft.**
   Climb the face to the right of the vertical outcropping.

4. **5.8, 20 ft.**
   Climb the face to the left of the horizontal crack.

5. **5.6, 20 ft.**
   In the center of the horizontal crack, climb the face.

6. **5.6, 20 ft.**
   Climb anywhere between the right end of the crack and the corner.

On the southwest (river)-facing side:

7. **5.9, 15 ft.**
   Around the corner, climb the lower face.

8. **5.9, 10 ft.**
   To the left of the low outcrop, climb the overhang.

9. **5.9, 10 ft.**
   Climb the center of the overhanging ledge.

## (West) Road-facing Side

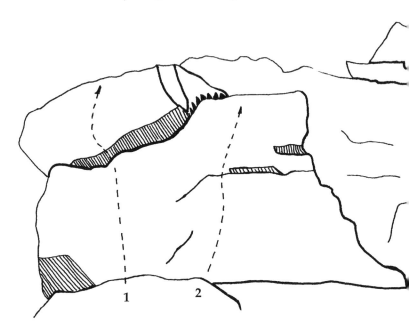

## (Southwest) River-facing Side

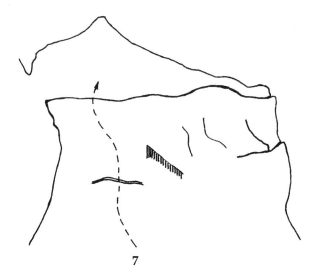

## (West) Road-facing Side

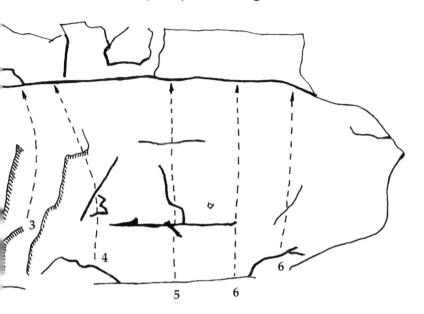

## (Southwest) River-facing Side

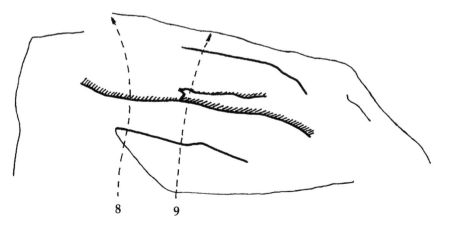

## (Southwest) River-facing Side

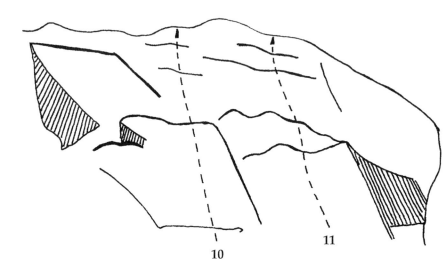

10   **5.9, 14 ft.**
     Climb the leaning slab.

11   **5.9, 14 ft.**
     Climb the face to the right of the leaning section.

12   **5.5, 12 ft.**
     Climb the face to the left of the diagonal crack. Variation: 5.8, 12 ft. Go straight up the face.

13   **5.8, 12 ft.**
     Climb the face under the pocket.

## (Southwest) River-facing Side

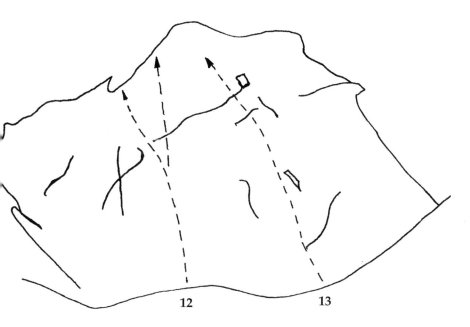

14  **5.10+, 20 ft.**
Climb the 9-foot overhang. Variation: Two routes with the same difficulty and heights.

15  **5.8, 18 ft.**
Starting by the low ripples, climb the face through the pocket.

16  **5.8, 18 ft.**
To the right of the block, climb the face.

17  **5.5, 18 ft.**
Climb the leaning face.

## (Southwest) River-facing Side

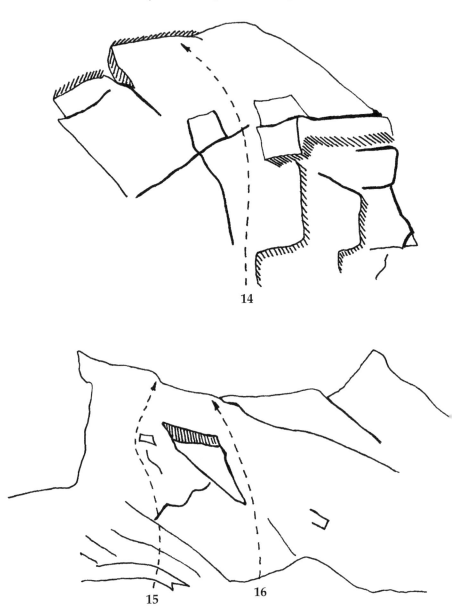

## (Southwest) River-facing Side

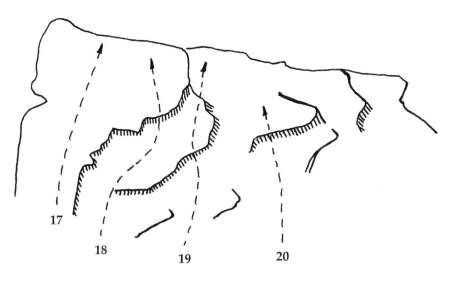

18  **5.5, 18 ft.**
    Climb over the vertical ledges on the leaning face.

19  **5.7, 18 ft.**
    Climb the overlapping slabs on the leaning face.

20  **5.8, 15 ft.**
    Climb the leaning slab.

### NEARBY AREAS

There is very little climbing other than the super-secret areas around Charlottesville. Give the local climbing stores a try.

### OTHER INFORMATION

I don't know of any decent campgrounds around Charlottesville, but you can head west on Route 64 toward Waynesboro to Rockfish Gap. From there you can go north on Skyline Drive or south on Blue Ridge Parkway.

• CHAPTER 29 •

# Tunstall's Tooth

Tunstall's Tooth is probably the tallest cliff in Virginia. Rising 225 feet over the James River, this hard limestone pinnacle offers good multi-pitch routes. First ascent of the A2 route on the river side was by James Scott and Fred Lang in 1970.

### DIRECTIONS

Tunstall's Tooth is located about 20 miles northwest of Lynchburg. Pass a town called Big Island and continue north on Route 501 for 2.6 miles. Tunstall's Tooth is the large cliff across the James River. Continue north past the Georgia Pacific Plant (stay away from the company's property) until you come to a bridge crossing the north river. There are good routes on both the river and the wooded sides of the tooth.

### ROUTE DESCRIPTIONS

I have not pictured any of the cliffs in this area. There are dozens of great routes here ranging from aid routes (which may have been bolted) to long free climbs.

## NEARBY AREAS

There is some rock at Otter Creek, only 5 to 8 miles north of Big Island along Blue Ridge Parkway. You are also very close to the Pedlar district of the George Washington National Forest.

## OTHER INFORMATION

Camp at Otter Creek by continuing north on Route 501 and turning right onto Blue Ridge Parkway.

• CHAPTER 30 •

# Goshen Pass Area

Normally known for its Boy Scout summer camp, Goshen Pass is another completely untapped climbing area with huge potential. Located in the heart of the Goshen–Little North Mountain Wildlife Management Area are a great variety of cliffs ranging up to 100 feet. Higher cliffs are only a bushwhack away up the ridges. After climbing, jump into one of the many trout-filled swimming holes along the Maury River. This guide offers only a brief glimpse at the area, and there is much more rock to be discovered. Special note: Use extra caution during hunting season, as this area is especially popular with the hunting crowd.

**DIRECTIONS**

From Highway 42, head west to Goshen and bear southwest onto Route 39. Go 4.4 miles on 39, where there is a dirt road/parking area on your right. Park here and cross the swinging bridge to reach the climbs on the east side of the Maury River. This is listed as Area A. First-timers or climbers who hate hiking to a climb should continue down the road for both a view of the ridges on the east side and climbs on the west side with shorter access. At 0.6 mile past the swinging bridge pull-off, you will come to a series of pull-offs for one or two vehicles. Close to the road at this first pull-off is Area B. Farther down the road is the Goshen Pass Wayside, a larger parking area. Continue 0.2 mile to a pull-off close to the point where the Laurel Run spills into the Maury River. This is Area C, the best spot for newcomers to begin.

## ROUTE DESCRIPTIONS

### AREA A

Reachable by the swinging bridge, this area offers a 75- to 90-foot cliff face nearly half a mile long. Long cracks and blank spots are visible, and the area is a nice place to camp. Area A is not pictured.

### AREA B

This area has a variety of excellent faces (60 to 100 feet), overhangs (4-to 20-foot ceilings), and routes. Here you are limited only by how far up the ridge you want to hike. Without heading too far up the ridge, you can find many routes. I know of only a few named routes in this area, but I encountered many climbers here in the early eighties.

1  **Iron Man 5.10+, 60 ft.**
   From the base of the cube-shaped formation, climb the south-facing side of the block.

2  **Jimmie's Dihedral 5.8, 70 ft.**
   Climb the sharp edge of the dihedral.

**Area B**

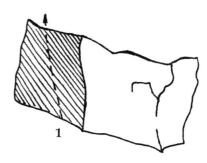

## AREA C

3 **5.10-, 55 ft.**
Climb the terraced overhang.

4 **5.6, 60 ft.**
Climb the leaning blocks.

5 **5.5, 65 ft.**
Climb the smooth face to the right of the leaning blocks.

**Area C**

## Area C

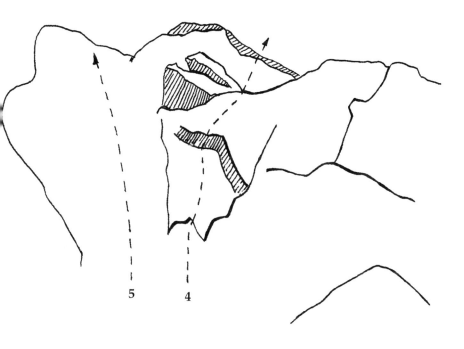

6  **5.7, 50 ft.**
   Another smooth face sandwiched between leaning blocks.

7  **5.4, 60 ft.**
   Easy face, often damp.

8  **The Grandpappy 5.12, 65 ft.**
   Climb the smooth face and the 12 foot overhang.

9  **5.9, 65 ft.**
   Climb the terraced overhangs to the right of The Grandpappy.

## Area C

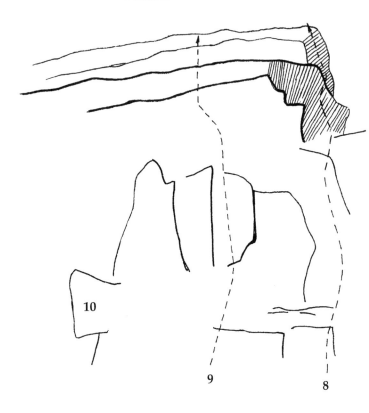

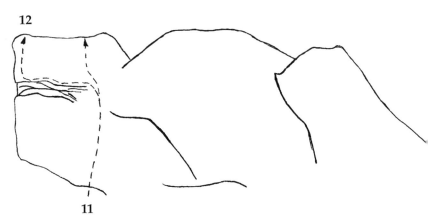

## Area C

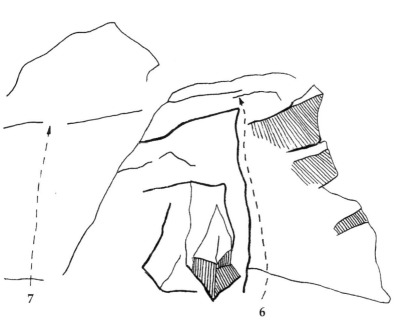

The face near the corner contains many 60- to 70-foot beginner's routes:

10   **5.1–5.4, 60–70 ft.**
     Climb anywhere. Beware of loose rocks.

Around the corner:

11   **5.10, 45 ft.**
     Tough overhang.

12   **5.6, 45 ft.**
     Climb to the underside of the overhang and avoid it to the left.

The cliff continues with routes ranging from 5.4 to 5.9 with some mossy areas and fewer overhangs.

## NEARBY AREAS

The closest areas to Goshen are Iron Gate, Eagle Rock, or Clifton Forge. Each of these areas is dealt with in other chapters. The Boy Scouts own some 100-foot cliffs, so write for permission to climb them and be prepared to be turned down. Stay off the Scout ranch unless you have written permission.

## OTHER INFORMATION

Look out for military jets. Fighter planes seem to roar through the pass, so don't panic if one tears through. Also, the Maury River tends to flood easily. Pay close attention to the weather. Camping in the area is free, and regulations are similar to those in most state parks.

• APPENDIX A •

# Other Possible Areas

Briefly, here are some other areas with basic directions. I have not been to all of these personally, so they do not come with any recommendations. There are essentially two types included here: areas that have good climbing but have longer approaches than the normal weekend climber would be willing to make, and areas that are rumored either by other backpackers/climbers or by trail guides to have cliffs.

**Hardscramble Knob, Bald Ridge Cliffs, Chimney Hollow, North Mountain, and Elliot Knob.** All are in the Ramsey Draft Wilderness Area, about 19 miles northwest of Staunton. Good climbs, but they generally involve rugged hikes of over 5 miles.

**Huckleberry Cliff and Naked Creek Falls.** No trails lead to these spots, but they are directly below Skyline Drive mile marker 53.3.

**Big Rock Falls.** An 8-mile death march to the falls from Milam Gap, Skyline Drive mile marker 52.5.

**Pinnacles of Dan.** Located along the Blue Ridge Parkway in Patrick County, close to North Carolina.

**Rocky Knob and Rock Gorge.** Also located along the Blue Ridge Parkway. Rocky Knob has a campground with the same name.

**Bear Cliff.** From Blacksburg, go west on Route 460 past Newport to 700. Turn right to Mountain Lake Hotel and park there. This is private property. The owners welcome backpackers and hikers, but get permission before climbing.

**Stone Mountain.** Located southwest of Big Stone Gap.

**Waterfall Mountain.** Part of the Massanutten group, near Elizabeth Furnace.

**Cascades.** Near Pembrooke in Thomas Jefferson National Forest.

**Pine Mountain.** Also in Thomas Jefferson National Forest.

**Flat Top and Fallingwater Cascades.** Located northwest of Bedford.

**Bullrun Mountain.** Once one of the great areas of Virginia climbing, it is now all on private property. Do not go there. Contact the Access Fund for information. There is little chance of this area being reopened in our lifetime. Maybe our grandkids will be able to climb here.

**Dark Hollow Falls and Tanner Ridge.** Off Skyline Drive and close by Big Meadows.

**Rocky Mount Trail.** At Skyline Drive mile marker 76.2. It is a 7-mile hike to the rocky ridge top.

**Comer's Rock.** Near Mount Rogers Recreation Area, by a campground with the same name.

**Balcony Falls.** Located close to Glasgow. Take Route 130 west; go left on 759, then left on 782. Park at Locher Tract.

**Devil's Marbleyard.** Years ago, I was told that this was a great bouldering area. It has a field of sandstone rubble, some small cliffs, and a waterfall. It can be reached by taking Route 130 west to 759. Turn left onto 781. The marked trailhead is on your left.

**White Rocks Gap.** Located near Sherando Lake.

If any of these areas are okay for climbing, let me know.

• APPENDIX B •

# Rules, Regulations, Addresses, YDS Rating System, and Other Useful Information

Here are some basic rules and advice to follow.
- Remember to hang your food to protect it from wild animals.
- Do not feed wild animals. You never know how they will react.
- Beware of ticks (which carry Rocky Mountain spotted fever and Lyme disease) and mice (which carry the hantavirus).
- Many of the trees in the forests have been damaged by hurricanes and gypsy moths. These trees are waiting to fall on unsuspecting hikers. Watch where you camp.
- Several bodies have been found in Shenandoah National Park, and two hikers were killed in 1996. Watch out for yourself and others.
- Some trails do not allow bikes or dogs. Check ahead of time.
- Be extra careful during hunting season. Wear an orange vest or hat if possible.
- Filter or boil your water. The clear springs and streams are full of deadly bacteria.

**SHENANDOAH NATIONAL PARK AND SKYLINE DRIVE**
The park is located an hour and a half west of Washington, D.C., in the heart of the Appalachian Mountains. Long recognized as one of the more beautiful areas of the country, this area was reclaimed (stolen) from farmers and settlers in 1935. The park includes about 200,000 acres with well over 500 miles of trails. The trails and every

trail intersection are well marked. The park has several entrances, but the main ones are Front Royal, Thornton Gap, Swift Run Gap, and Rockfish Gap. The main and only road running through the park is the 105-mile-long Skyline Drive.

**Transportation.** Portions of Skyline Drive close at night during hunting season and when the weather gets bad, but the drive is usually open. The speed limit is 35 mph and is enforced. The southernmost end of Skyline Drive links up with Blue Ridge Parkway.

**Weather.** As in most mountainous regions, the weather here can change without notice. Snowstorms are not uncommon even in the late spring. Be prepared for the worst.

**Fees.** There is a $10 fee per vehicle, which covers you for a week. A better value is to buy a yearly pass for $20 or a pass for all national parks for $50. Many climbers whine about the fees, but dollar for dollar, this is your best entertainment value.

**Facilities.** Most park facilities close between Labor Day and Memorial Day. All the following areas have picnic spots, and most have water during the summer months (the number refers to the Skyline Drive mile marker):
- Dickey Ridge Visitor Center and toilets, 4.6
- Elkwallow Wayside, store and restaurant, 24.1
- Panorama Restaurant, food, water, and toilets, 31.5
- Pinnacles, toilets, 36.7
- Skyland Lodge and Restaurant, food, water, and toilets, 41.7
- Harry Bryd Visitor Center and Big Meadows Campground (reservations required), lodges, cabins, wayside, restaurant, store, wood, ice, showers, and washers and dryers, 51
- Lewis Mountain Campground (first come, first served), cabins, camp store, wood, ice, showers, and washers and dryers, 57.6
- South River, toilets, 62.8
- Loft Mountain Information Center, campground (first come, first served), restaurant, and store, 79.5
- Dundo Group Campground (reservations required), 83.7

**Camping.** For camping options, see the facilities list or get a backcountry permit at any ranger station (or by writing). You can camp almost anywhere in the park. Certain areas with heavy traffic are closed to camping. Camping in parking areas or within sight of the trails is not allowed. The rangers will go over the current rules when you get your permit. Some trailheads and park entrances have self-registration stations, but the park is phasing them out.

**Other.** No glass is allowed in the park.

**Contact Information.** Shenandoah National Park, 3655 U.S. Highway 211 E, Luray, Virginia 22835-9036; (540) 999-3500. http://www.nps.gov/shen/#camp.

## THE BLUE RIDGE PARKWAY

The Blue Ridge Parkway is a scenic 470-mile-long road linking Shenandoah and Great Smoky Mountain National Parks. Like Skyline Drive, the parkway is open year-round, but it can be closed in bad weather. The trails are well marked. About 220 miles of the parkway are in the state of Virginia.

**Fees.** The parkway is free. There is a $10-per-night fee in the campgrounds.

**Transportation.** Each mile on the parkway is marked by a milepost. The speed limit is 45, but certain areas are marked 35.

**Facilities.** Most Blue Ridge Parkway campgrounds are open from May through October. Several are open year-round. Unlike in Shenandoah National Park, you cannot camp along the Blue Ridge Parkway trails, but you are permitted to camp along Forest Service trails. Permits are required for the backcountry areas. All the following campgrounds have water and toilets (the number refers to the mile marker):

- Otter Creek Campground and Lodge, 60.9
- Peaks of Otter Campground, 86.1
- Roanoke Mountain Campground, 120.3
- Rocky Knob Campground, backcountry camping and cabins, 169.0

**Other Information.** Fires are permitted in designated spaces. At the park superintendent's discretion, "No Fire Periods" can be established. Swimming is illegal along Blue Ridge Parkway.

**Contact Information.** Blue Ridge Parkway, 400 BB&T Building, Asheville, NC, 28801; (704) 298-0398. http://www.nps.gov/blri/

## GEORGE WASHINGTON AND THOMAS JEFFERSON NATIONAL FORESTS

These two national forests take up 1.9 million acres of land in both West Virginia and Virginia. They offer over 2,000 miles of trails, with the Appalachian Trail traveling 336 miles through them. Take a map and compass with you, and learn how to use them. The trails are not always well marked and it is easy to become lost or hike in the wrong direction.

**No Trace.** The national forests have a no-trace policy, which essentially means that you must leave no trace when camping. This means no littering or otherwise impacting the forest in any way.

**Campgrounds.** Camp anywhere. There are many official campgrounds, some with fees and some without. Follow the rules posted in each area, especially the "No Trespassing" signs. Also remember to camp out of sight of the Appalachian Trail. Do not expect the shelters around the Appalachian Trail to have space for you. They are almost always filled with through-hikers.

**Contact Information.** George Washington and Thomas Jefferson National Forests, 5162 Valleypointe Parkway, Roanoke, VA 24019; (540) 265-6054. http://www.fs.fed.us/rec...r8_georgewashington.html

## VIRGINIA'S STATE PARKS

Virginia has a fantastic state park system. This guidebook cannot go into detail on Virginia's parks, but I'll give you some basics. Most areas have fees for either camping or entry. Some have provisions for wilderness (i.e., free) camping. The rules are really no different from those of the national forests or national parks.

**Contact Information.** Department of Conservation and Recreation, Governor Street, Suite 302, Richmond, VA 23219; (804) 786-1712. http://www.state.va.us/~dcr/parks

For camping reservations, call 1-800-933-PARK.

## THE APPALACHIAN TRAIL

The Appalachian Trail is the famous trail leading from Maine to Georgia. More of the Appalachian Trail passes through Virginia than any other state. Follow the rules of the park that the trail passes through and camp out of sight of the trail. The Potomac Appalachian

Trail Club and the Roanoke Appalachian Trail Club can provide excellent maps and detailed information on the trail.

**Contact Information.** The Appalachian Trail Conference, PO Box 807, Harpers Ferry, WV 25425; Potomac Appalachian Trail Club, 118 Park Street., SE, Vienna, VA 22180; Roanoke Appalachian Trail Club, PO Box 12282, Roanoke, VA 24024.

For more information on climbing areas, check out the bibliography, read rec.climbing on the Internet, or call a nearby university and ask for the outdoor activities group. Most schools have good groups, but the members and interest level vary from year to year. You could also check out the web pages for the Potomac Appalachian Trail Club by doing a keyword search for "PATC" or check out the web pages of any of the many climbing and outdoor magazines on the Internet by doing a keyword search. Or you can hang around climbing areas.

## THE YOSEMITE DECIMAL SYSTEM (YDS)
### RATINGS OF TECHNICAL DIFFICULTY

**Class 1** Walking or easy hiking
**Class 2** Difficult hiking; scrambling and balance required
**Class 3** Climbing; use of hands required
**Class 4** Exposed climbing; a fall could cause injury; ropes and belays may be used
**Class 5** Technical climbing with ropework and protection required

> **5.0–5.4** Beginners' routes
> **5.5, 5.6** Intermediate routes; moderately difficult
> **5.7** Requires advanced climbing skills
> **5.8–5.10** Difficult; technically and physically challenging for the weekend climber
> **5.11–5.13** Severely difficult; requires daily training and commitment
> **5.14** Highest current rating; world class climbers only.

*Note:* Beginning at 5.10, routes are further subdivided into 5.10a, 5.10b, and so on, each letter indicating a slightly higher degree of difficulty.

# Bibliography

**BOOKS**

Adkins, Leonard M. *A Guide to the Trails of the Blue Ridge Parkway.* Chapel Hill: University of North Carolina Press, 1992.

*Appalachian Trail Guide.* Vol. 6, *Maryland to Northern Virginia.* Edited by Jean Golightly. Vienna, VA: Potomac Appalachian Trail Club, 1986.

———.Vol. 7, *Shenandoah National Park.* Edited by Jean Golightly. Vienna, VA: Potomac Appalachian Trail Club, 1991.

———. Vol. 8, *Central and Southwest Virginia.* Edited by Jack Albright. Harpers Ferry, WV: Appalachian Trail Conference, 1991.

Canter, Ronald and Kathy Canter. *Nearby Climbing Areas.* 1980. (I've never been able to find a copy of this guide, but it is rumored to have great route information on many obscure areas around Washington, D.C.)

*Carderock: Past and Present.* Edited by Selma I. Hamel. Washington, DC: Potomac Appalachian Trail Club, 1990. (Mostly deals with the popular Maryland area, but also has good information on some small areas in Virginia.)

*Climbers' Guide to the Great Falls of the Potomac.* Edited by James A. Eakin. Vienna, VA: Potomac Appalachian Trail Club, 1985.

Conners, John A. *Shenandoah National Park: An Interpretive Guide.* Blacksburg, VA: MacDonald & Woodward, 1988. (A good geological guide to the park.)

deHart, Allen. *The Trails of Virginia: Hiking the Old Dominion.* Chapel Hill: University of North Carolina Press, 1995.
*Guide to the Massanutten Mountain: George Washington National Forest.* Edited by James W. Denton. Washington, DC: Potomac Appalachian Trail Club, 1982.
*Hiking Guide to the Pedlar District: George Washington National Forest.* Edited by Michael T. Shoemaker. Washington, DC: Potomac Appalachian Trail Club, 1990.
Wuertz-Schaefer, Karin. *Hiking Virginia's National Forests.* Old Saybrook, CT: Globe Pequot Press, 1994.

## MAGAZINES

*American Alpine Journal* 17 (1970): 139. (Article on Tunstall's Tooth.)
*Rock and Ice* 8, (May 1985) (Great article on Old Rag Mountain by the master of Virginia climbing, Greg Collins).

**ABOUT THE AUTHOR**

Jeff Watson is a native Virginian, avid mountaineer, and 17-year veteran of rock climbing. He lives in Burke, Virginia.